The Story Experience

Jane B. Wilson

The Scarecrow Press, Inc.
Metuchen, N.J., & London  1979

The passage on pp. x-xi is reprinted from The
World of Washington Irving, copyright © 1944,
1950 by Van Wyck Brooks, renewed © 1972 by
Gladys Brooks, by permission of the publishers,
E. P. Dutton.

Library of Congress Cataloging in Publication Data

Wilson, Jane B   1914-
   The story experience.

   Bibliography: p.
   Includes index.
   1. Story-telling--United States. 2. Oral tradition--
United States. I. Title.
LB1042.W55   808.5'43   79-13888
ISBN 0-8108-1224-X

For Saza Peck

who told her story well —
and with love

CONTENTS

vi   Table of Contents

Introduction

THE ORAL TRADITION

The exact number of human tongues, languages and dialects in use around the world is unknown. A recent estimate places the figure, ancient and modern, between eight and ten thousand. The Library of the British and Foreign Bible Society in London contains Bible translations in some two thousand languages. A majority of obscure spoken languages and dialects is unrecorded in written or printed form to any significant extent.

One fact stands out: oral communication among mankind antedated by millenia the art of writing. Over the centuries, written and spoken languages have grown side by side, each complementing the other. Numerous classics of ancient and medieval literature were transmitted by storytellers, folk singers, balladeers, troubadours, and wandering minstrels, from generation to generation, before literary geniuses decided to preserve them in writing. Examples are the Iliad and the Odyssey, Aesop's Fables, the Scandinavian sagas, the Norse-Icelandic Eddas, the Gesta Romanorum, the medieval beast-epic Reynard the Fox, and the Morte d'Arthur, Beowulf, and Everyman in English legends. Most often, myths were sung to music to enhance their dramatic qualities. And what is modern opera except stories set to music and acted out?

Migratory peoples have insured a wide geographical distribution of folktales and ballads. Comparisons by professional folklorists have revealed over and over again that close parallels exist among widely-scattered races in the stories they tell and the folksongs they sing. As one instance, the story of Cinderella is found in Icelandic literature a thousand years old, and similar tales have turned up in Bohemia, England, France, Russia and elsewhere. Again, a common theme in German folktales is about a man who slept for many years, inspiring Washington Irving to write the

story of Rip Van Winkle, a lazy Dutchman living in a small
village along the Hudson River.   A leading American folklorist, Mody Boatright, has termed such stories "folk travel-
ers. "

    Nowhere is this great melting pot of folklore more in
evidence than in America.   Immigrants from around the
world--and particularly from the British Isles and western
Europe--brought with them their native tales and songs.   As
time passed, the New World atmosphere caused gradual modi-
fications until the lore became Americanized.   Swiss and
Swede, Hungarian and Irish, Dutch and Spanish, Finn and
Dane living together directly influenced each other, as they
exchanged Old World lore, leading in the end to distinctly
American forms.

    At the same time, tightly-knit ethnic groups in Amer-
ica have retained stories and songs brought with them from
abroad.   Thus, we have Scots in the Southern highlands,
Scandinavians in the Dakotas, the "Dutch" in Pennsylvania,
French Acadians in the Louisiana bayou country, Spanish-
speaking people along the Mexican border, Yankee seafarers
on the New England coast, and other distinctive elements in
a vast country preserving their unique cultures.   This fact
is especially true where groups have remained somewhat iso-
lated and apart, not fully assimilated into the general population.

    Versions of fables told by Southern Negro slaves have
been discovered in Siam, India, Egypt, the Arab countries,
and South America.   In the South, the tales appear to have
been universally known long before they were recorded by
Joel Chandler Harris and other folklorists.   In nearly every
instance, their roots could be traced back to an African oral
tradition.

    In brief, it could be said that, strictly interpreted,
little of American folklore is indigenous, except that of the
Amerindians which was present when the white man arrived.

    A fascinating branch of folklore is animal mythology.
Since time immemorial, man has tended to create animals
in his own image, to imagine non-human creatures with the
power of speech and human beings with the ability to understand the language of beasts and birds.   Perhaps originating
in a primeval sense of kinship with lower members of the
great animal kingdom--of which man is merely the highest

embodiment--the race has for thousands of years related
beast fables for purposes of allegory, satire, and recreation.
With the advent of recorded literature appear Aesop's Fables,
telling of animals that talk and act like human beings; the
Biblical episodes of Eve's talking serpent and Balaam's talk-
ing ass; the Arabian Nights, abounding in beast tales; and
Pliny's Natural History, describing, for example, dolphins
carrying human riders.   American specimens include Uncle
Remus' Brer Rabbit stories and Mark Twain's "Blue Jay
Yarn. "

        In ancient and medieval tales, mythological creatures
include the dragon, with its lion's claws, eagle's wings, serpent's tail, and fiery breath; the griffin, a cross between a
lion and an eagle; the unicorn, a monster with a long horn
jutting forth from the center of its forehead, with the legs
of an antelope and the body of a horse; and Pegasus, a flying horse.

        To match such fabulous fauna of the Old World, Amer-
ica can offer the hodag, the whiffle-poofle, the sidehill gou-
ger, the squonk, the cactus cat, the dingmaul, the gumberoo,
the hoop-snake, the wampus, the swamp auger, and many
others.   A source of recent scary stories coming out of the
Pacific Northwest is the Yeti or Sasquatch, a huge, humanoid
seven-foot-tall creature, akin to the Abominable Snowman of
Tibet.

        Typically, real or imaginary beasts in ancient and
medieval folklore possessed religious significance, reflected
primitive superstitions (or scientific ignorance), or served
to illustrate moral lessons.   The phenomenal creatures that
developed in America assumed many different characteristics.
The extraordinary lore relating to animal, bird, fish, insect,
and plant life formed in America has few, if any, rivals for
vivid color, inventiveness, humor, and originality.

        The American tall tale and apocryphal biology may
have had their beginning in the year 1000, when it is related
that Thorwald, son of Eric the Red, was fatally wounded in
Nova Scotia by a Uniped or One-Footer.   Jacques Cartier in
the sixteenth century also brought back from his Canadian
explorations reports of a land peopled by a race of one-legged
folk.   Near the same time, Christopher Columbus made contributions to legend by reporting after his return home that
he himself had seen three sirens leaping about in the sea
and "at a distance there were men with one eye only, and

others with faces like dogs, who were man-eaters"--a whopper picked up from Haitian Indians. In 1712, Cotton Mather reported to the Royal Society of London that the steel in a broad-axe had broken when bitten by a rattlesnake. A leading chronicler of New England folklore, Richard Dorson, notes that such wildly improbable, but widely prevalent, stories were the fruits of naive superstition and pious gullibility, rather than attempts at humor.

A distinctive characteristic of American oral folklore and humor is the tall tale. Such stories are handed down from one generation to the next, polished and improved by time. The tales turn up in all regions of the country and have many points of similarity. One authority, Walter Blair, has defined the tall tale as "an exuberant combination of fact with outrageous fiction. " Frequently there is a tiny grain of truth somewhere in the most improbable yarn. In fact, it has been suggested that the improving on actual happenings rather than outright lying is the distinguishing feature of the tall tale. Nevertheless, this type of story deals frankly with marvels, with the remarkable or prodigious.

J. Frank Dobie, another recognized expert, pointed out that the genuine narrator of tall tales considers himself an artist. He knows what he is prevaricating about and his listeners know also, unless they are greenhorns or tenderfeet--in which case, of course, they are fair game. Therefore, the narrator does not pretend to fool either himself or his audience. His object is amusement and recreation, and he may need no further excuse for existence.

Perhaps it is the great spaces and wide frontiers that have stimulated the growth of the American tall tale. Reaching back into history, one can imagine how the totally different flora and fauna of the New World must have affected pioneers from the Old. Van Wyck Brooks, writing of "the wondrous West, " as he called it, in the period around 1800, made these comments:

> "One heard of watermelons as large as houses and trees on Miami river in which honey grew, springs of rum and brandy that gushed from the Kentucky hills and flax-plants that bore woven cloth in their branches. With these humorous yarns were mingled others that might have been true; and how was a credulous Easterner to draw the line? Was there not really perhaps a hoop-snake that spun through the swamps like a

wheel, a whip-snake that killed cattle with the lashing
of its tail and a serpent that exhaled a fatal gas?
These tall tales that crossed the mountains were true
as intimations that almost anything indeed might happen in the West. The West possessed the largest riv-
ers; and were not the storms more terrible there,
were not the bears more dangerous than anywhere
else? Moreover, the true frontiersman, whom one
sometimes saw in Philadelphia, striding through the
streets with the step of an Achilles, suggested that
he could manage the storms and the bears. No tales
about the West could ever seem tall to anyone who
saw him with a rifle. He could perforate a milk-pail
half a mile away, he could enlarge the tin eye of the
cock on the steeple, he could split a bullet on a razor
at a hundred paces and cut the string of a flag at three
hundred yards. This William Tell was a walking and
visible legend" (The World of Washington Irving [New
York: E. P. Dutton, 1944).

During the nineteenth century yarns of hunting, fishing
and outdoor pursuits were exceedingly popular. During that
era, such folk heroes as Davy Crockett, Daniel Boone, Andy
Jackson, Mike Fink, Kit Carson, Wild Bill Hickok, Sam Bass,
Buffalo Bill and "Johnny Appleseed" (John Chapman) came
into prominence. To these the folk added such fictional su-
permen as Paul Bunyan, John Henry, Tony Beaver, and Pecos
Bill. Bold men created bold myths, and America became a
land of marvelous stories, both true and false, revolving a-
round heroic figures.

Creative storytellers in our population include farmers,
who have never been modest in adding their bit to the great
American brag; Western cowboys, who with many nights to
spend sitting around campfires and ranch houses have had
ample time to give their imaginations free rein; and the lum-
berjacks, river boatmen, railroad workers, Indian fighters,
Ozark mountaineers--all of whom have contributed generously
to the great Archive of American Folklore assembled by the
Library of Congress. Meanwhile, as Ben Clough remarks,
"our weather stories, hunting stories, fish stories, impossible yarns, and sheer hoaxes go on. The great American
liar is of no era, and of all, he is immortal."

Stephen Vincent Benét, who drew extensively upon
folklore for his own stories and poems, once wrote: "It's
always seemed to me that legends and yarns and folk tales

are as much a part of the real history of the country as proclamations and provisos and constitutional amendments. The legends and yarns get down to the roots of the people-- they tell a good deal about what people admire and want, about what sort of people they are. You can explain America in terms of formal history; and you can also explain it in terms of Rip Van Winkle and Paul Bunyan, of Casey Jones and Davy Crockett--not the Crockett whose actual exploits are in the history books, but the Crockett who was a legend during his lifetime, the frontiersman up on his hind legs" (Carl Carmer, "Folklore," Compton's Encyclopedia [1973 ed.], vol. 8, pp. 304-5).

Crockett, incidentally, had an active political career, and politics has produced a special breed of storytellers-- long a fertile field for American humorists. A few leaders in state-craft have been celebrated for their storytelling ability, but a majority of professional politicians has regarded humor as a dangerous two-edged weapon. Two striking exceptions, Benjamin Franklin and Abraham Lincoln, were both famous for humorous anecdotes. In recent times, Adlai Stevenson and Jack Kennedy made effective use of humorous stories in political campaigns and on other occasions. Lincoln was, of course, our most noted raconteur and yarnspinner.

The importance of oral storytelling in America was recognized by an English observer nearly ninety years ago. The very discerning Andrew Lang wrote in 1889, "All over the land men are eternally 'swopping stories' at bars, and in the long, endless journeys by railway and steamer. How little, comparatively, the English 'swop stories.' The stories thus collected in America are the subsoil of American literary humor, a rich soil in which the plant grows with vigor and puts forth fruit and flowers."

Many adjectives descriptive of American oral folk humor have been used: boisterous, racy, irreverent, earthy, exuberant, zestful, Rabelaisian, full of gusto, close to the soil. Folk humor is undoubtedly closer to the mass of the people than any written literature. At the same time, the folklore heritage has strongly influenced more formal literature. One of the first major writers to tap this rich stream was Mark Twain. Much of Twain's success as a writer lay in his ability to remember and use the Mississippi and Missouri lore he had heard as a boy and a young man. Scarcely less indebted to oral traditions were Washington Irving, Herman Melville, Nathaniel Hawthorne, James Fenimore Cooper, Henry W. Longfellow, Bret Harte, and numerous lesser figures--limiting the field to the nineteenth century alone.

The skillful and talented storyteller has universal appeal, at every cultural level from the lowliest illiterate to the most highly educated sophisticate, from the youngest to the oldest. How strong the oral tradition is in our culture has been demonstrated by such performers as Charles Dickens, Mark Twain, Irvin S. Cobb, Alexander Woollcott, Charles Laughton, Bennett Cerf, and Carl Sandburg, all of whom were immensely popular on the stage as readers and storytellers, as well as in their published works.

Clearly there will always be a place for the verbal artist alongside the scribe who prefers to commit his thoughts to paper.

* * * * * *

Jane Bliss Wilson comes near being uniquely qualified to write The Story Experience, passing on to her colleagues in the storytelling field a wealth of experience gathered over the years from practice and teaching. When she received the Grolier Foundation Award, in 1975, for a librarian "who had made an unusual contribution to the stimulation and guidance of reading by children and young people," the citation read as follows:

> "To Jane Bliss Wilson in recognition of more than three decades of creative leadership in library service to children and young adults. As a librarian, a supervisor at both the district and state levels, a teacher, and a storyteller, she has used unparalleled creativity in motivating the development of library programs for the young. An enthusiasm and love of books, combined with scholarly knowledge of her field and a determined sense of leadership, have allowed Jane B. Wilson to make a contribution to librarianship which serves as an inspiration to all who know and have worked with her. Programs established through her leadership will serve as a challenge to those who follow her."

Miss Wilson's career has been amazingly rich and varied. She originated one of the first radio children's programs in the country. Later, while a children's librarian on the Detroit Public Library staff, she became a member of the National Story League, to be on call as one of its city-wide storytellers; a storyteller in residence for the Detroit Saturday School to aid disadvantaged and foreign-born children living in the inner-city; a storyteller for the Chinese Sunday School; conductor of the first radio program for children under the sponsorship of the Detroit Public Library; and conductor of one of the first preschool story hours in the United States.

After her return to North Carolina in 1940, Miss Wilson served successively as young adult librarian for the Durham Public Library; children's librarian of the Olivia Raney (Raleigh) Public Library (where she developed a popular children's radio program); head librarian of the R. J. Reynolds High School in Winston-Salem; the first supervisor of Durham elementary school libraries; creator of the first local educational television sustaining story program for boys and girls, from Chapel Hill; director of libraries in the Durham City Schools; and finally, until her retirement in 1975, the first public library consultant for children's services for the North Carolina State Library.

Miss Wilson has also played an active role in the American and North Carolina Library Associations, serving as president of the latter. She has been a consultant on storytelling for various institutions and a consultant for the H. W. Wilson Company's Children's Catalog. Her teaching assignments have included visiting lectureships in books for children and young people at Duke University, the University of North Carolina, University of Maryland, University of Kentucky, and East Carolina University. During the summer of 1977 she directed a three-week storytelling institute for the University of North Carolina at Greensboro's Division of Library Science, in which she had taught previously as a guest lecturer.

All of the foregoing extraordinary background, and more, plus a highly creative mind and imagination, are brought to bear by Miss Wilson in presenting this important contribution to a vital area of librarianship.

ROBERT B. DOWNS

Chapter One

"THE BELL OF ATRI"

For some it may be difficult to remember when the
yearning to share a story began to make itself felt. For
one, it came with the tolling of a bell, ringing out injustice
in an anonymous tale centuries old. The forceful, simple
Italian story, "The Bell of Atri," rescued by Carolyn Sherwin Bailey early in the twentieth century, rang out a grave
injury to an old but faithful horse abandoned by his ungrate-
ful master.[1]* The message of the bell so stirred a young
listener that for a lifetime the bell of Atri stood as the sym-
bol of advocacy for childhood. The clear, first ringing served
an impressive summons to make known to boys and girls stories from many times and places. The call of the bell was
for a commitment to awaken youth to the joys of understanding and compassion. Through such a story--not a preach-
ment--it was thought that life could be studied; that a listening experience could show a way and encourage youngsters to
explore, observe, and stand tall in the doing. Thus, one life
was gently molded, and another storyteller was off and telling.

The pledge was renewed at the savage hiss of the great
White Cobra recalling the days of Bappa Rawal[2]; when the
inchworm listened to, and measured, the song of the nightingale "until he inched out of sight."[3] The yearning grew,
nurtured by the bat-poet's eager recitation of his own verse.[4]
These sounds were longed for and when they leaped out to
tell a story, listeners were born. The brass band on Mulberry Street, according to Marco, "should have someone to
hear it...."[5] No medium can pass on better these memorable messages than the human voice recreating aloud the
glowing pictures that are written. The bell of Atri was still
ringing when Esteban's ghost wailed in the chimney[6]; when
Billy Nell Kewley "could draw as sweet music from the fid-
dle as any fiddler of Man."[7] What excitement rang with the

---

*All sources cited briefly (usually with just author's last name)
in chapter notes or in the text are given in full in the Bibliography at the back of the book.

bell when Tieg heard the miller's wee Cassie singing outside his cabin on Saint Stephen's Eve![8] What astonishment and gay humor were set in motion when the stool said, "Fantastic, isn't it? ... Imagine, a talking yam!"[9] And so it goes: hundreds and hundreds of happenings woven by the great and the good. How could anyone sit idly by? A tale is for telling.

The listening experience, however, comes along before the bell may be fully obeyed, since the teller of tales is first a listener. It takes a lifetime for the storyteller to hear all the stories told by trees in a wood; by birds in those trees; the rain and the tree frog; squirrels on the branches; the bee on a blossom. Each adds, canto after canto, to a melodic ballad that continues night and day. The thunder above the wood is heard by the oak, and this tale is mighty. From nightly visiting owls come screechings of furtiveness abroad, or prophesies of sensational deeds.

The house in the wood blends its sounds: a medley of telephone bell, furnace and freezer motors; clocks striking to the rhythm of the cars on the road beyond, dashing against the rain. Winter brings the silence of the snow; the footsteps of the shivering field mice as they search for a door left partially open; the knock of the woodpecker and the jay as they open sunflower seeds against the feeder. These, too, are the sounds and silences woven into the tales of life. Poets have heard them all.

These words come like music--and color--and men and women and children listen. Listeners see again their own experiences (remembered folk and places) and are reassured. They see new lands, hear other voices, and learn, because the speaker brings news. The listener is caught and whirled into the tale, living for a single moment in the good, the great, the naughty, the lost. The teller's voice awakens dreams and spins stuff for thought; incites to contemplation.

Sometimes the listeners move away, busy with their learning. Even so, the storyteller may speak, giving back the tale to the wind, and to the trees, for them to weep.

Everyone complains of the lack of communication, of the failure to understand the what and why and how: employer fails to make clear the command; employee is unable to get across fears or unrest. The parent does not take time to listen; the child--defeated--cannot speak. To stretch and make room for the thoughts, ideas, or goals of others, all must learn to listen. It may be true that hearing is the one sense that comes full-blown when life begins; it can be the last to survive.

Those who wish to recall the languages and the literatures of the past should look to the learning of the skills of storytelling. With practice and care, the skill may become an art. How to? Let the story lift and flow; let it laugh and cry. Take the best tales; take pride in our human possession of such wealth; take joy in the delight of giving it away. Give tales to all to hold as strength against the days of loneliness and despair. Be ready so all may thrill to the best that has been thought, spoken, written since the world began. Speak to any listener anywhere: on lawns, in yards and gardens; on steps, in schools; near libraries and churches. Use any medium carrying the human voice. All people crave the new, the old, the known, the thrilling unknown--any opportunity to live through others.

Out of the 1960's came the truth of what risks it means not to listen. It took a lot of getting used to, the fury of youth. Deep in the heart one agreed with the young screaming for honesty, for fair-dealing--for an end to war. So often before youth has spoken to the ears of those too high to notice them. But children spoke out, and miracle of miracles, the world listened. Serenity may have come too soon--young clamorers grew tired--but for a little while most ears did hear.

It is difficult to speak and to listen at the same time. The shock of youthful protest finally helped calm to come, and with it, memory; a need to think and then to speak. But wounds went deep, and from the struggle came the courage to put into words a cry of yearning for dignity and knowledge. With the desire to set aright one great wrong came the later pleading for heritage, for roots, for a starting point. What better place to begin than where Man began? The true beginnings were in language shared among men, women, and children in the firelight in front of caves, beneath torches in keep and castle; in market place, in temple, beneath marble columns; on porches in the twilight, at the noon-hour in shops and stores; in churches, schools, and libraries: wherever storytellers spun their yarns.

Those who tell tales are both listeners and speakers. They have heard and remembered. The folklore of all the various cultures prove the similarities in development of all

races. The stories are customs arising from needs: to
speak, to touch; to allay fears provoked by violent nature
and to explain her abundance; to identify with a Being greater
than oneself; to shape this Being in one's own image. The
overwhelming need is to know oneself and one's group and to
place one in the world--and to seek out others with whom to
share.

"Cinderella," "Tom Tit Tot," "The Frog Prince," and
"Little Red Riding Hood" are some of the stories that portray
universal attitudes and responses. Bettelheim has enumerated
the variants of several of the better-known folktales, and his
analyses give ample substantiation to the belief that they are
repetitions of world-wide needs. Bettelheim discusses how
these needs were perceived and remembered; how the problems they represented were attacked for resolution via stories. The stories he used as examples and discussed at length
all manifest to the listener a means of release from private
fears or wonderings; that the stories did so is one of the main
themes of his book.

Another value of listening to stories is that it gives
additional opportunities for children to hear words and, with
these words, to increase the power to think. The child who
hears little conversation is often limited in vocabulary. Children who converse only with their peers learn fewer new
words than children who are exposed to much wider and more
mature relationships.

The child should be allowed to imagine without imped-
iments the settings to the stories being unfolded. When the
narrator has selected a tale worth the telling and has visu-
alized the action, truly experiencing the story line in advance
of delivery, the listener is not hampered by weak spots.

Imagination, freed, may deal with nuances of a story
in a way immensely enriched by the memory of experiences
both personal and vicarious. Free of the thought that the
storyteller may hesitate, may forget, one may relax and attend
to the development of the plot--even leaping ahead, in an instant to invent what lies ahead. One is free to go into the
tale and become challenger, villain, or bystander. One may
listen for new sounds, new words and phrases that please the
ear, tickle the fancy, touch one with humor. As one, listening, becomes a part of the tale, its teller is stimulated and
recognizes a partner in the experience. Enjoyment is thus
enhanced for each.

Not only is the story important but also is the enthusiasm the storyteller takes to this shared experience. Here
the attitude and quality of the interpreter's prior listening,
reading, and learning show through each word and action,
each movement of the body. One may well ask which is the
more important, the story or the storyteller. Would that it
were the story: then there would be no lack in opportunities
for listening to a good tale. But the true storyteller, with
eyes, hands, body and voice (and all that mind and memory
can project), is the living instrument that directs and illu-
mines the narrative.

Many writers on the art of storytelling stress the part
played by music in the building of a storyteller's background.
They do so rightly since it is a part of the folk heritage, but
this discipline is only one aspect of the lesson to be learned.
During a storytelling demonstration for a news service recently, the teller was delighted to observe the excitement enjoyed by the young journalist-photographer as he went about
his assignment. Such enthusiasm is not difficult to understand since journalism came straight from the ancient newsgatherers, the storytellers. The folktale is a manifestation
of the tenets of reporting: Who, When, What, Where--and
sometimes Why and How: Kipling's six serving men. [10] The
young man was not so delighted with the antics of the storyteller (nor the merit of the story) as he was with the form
of the tale. To this he could relate, and another spokesman
for storytelling was born.

The honest directness of a simple tale is recognized
by the listener, and one is assured that the story is all-important and not some hidden rule, admonition, or moral.
One settles back to let the mind wander with the words upon
the ears. The storyteller is the interpreter for the audience,
but a true artist must listen to the wordless tale occurring
in the minds of the listeners. The task is great; the responsibility is two-fold. One must be aware of what the audience
may be seeing as the storyteller paints the word-pictures.
The narrator reaches back into personal experiences to imagine what the listener may be re-living, and often must be
careful to remember certain slight phrases that can be so
full of personal meaning.

In The Five Chinese Brothers, Claire Bishop tells of
the boat that "made for the open sea." A class of storytellers discussed what may pass through the minds of listeners
when this phrase is given its full share of emphasis. Slight

phrase it may be, but it suggests a delicious moment and re-
calls the vastness of oceans and the eternal fascination that
sea rhythms have for Man.

The listener remains a member of the group, but is
alone in sensing once again the salt spray, the undulation of
a vessel. Here emerges the true art of the storyteller--and
upon an inner canvas the listeners paint their thoughts; memories, and dreams. Here is another art: the listener retells
the story silently within, harvesting the images as they are
spoken. Because of the endless influence of the teller of
tales, one must speak sincerely--but first, one must listen
to that silent story the listener is "speaking." The storyteller must measure the tale as the inchworm measured the
nightingale's song.

NOTES

1. Bailey: "The Bell of Atri," pp. 78-84.

2. Kipling, Jungle Books: "The King's Ankus,"
pp. 123-148.

3. Lionni.

4. Jarrell.

5. Geisel (Dr. Seuss), And to Think....

6. Boggs and Davis: "The Tinker and the Ghost,"
pp. 97-108.

7. Sawyer, The Long Christmas: "Fiddler, Play
Fast, Play Faster," pp. 33-43.

8. Ibid. : "The Voyage of the Wee Red Cap,"
pp. 109-120. (Originally published in This Way to Christmas, Harper & Row, c1916, as "Barney's Tale of the Wee
Red Cap," pp. 28-42.)

9. Courlander and Herzog: "Talk," pp. 25-29.

10. Kipling, ed. Beecroft: pp. 383-384; a tailpiece
to "The Elephant's Child," "I keep six honest serving-men...."

Chapter Two

THE ABC OF STORYTELLING

Near the center of Michelangelo's ceiling in the Sistine Chapel in Rome, God is reaching out with a finger to Adam, creating Man. Whatever the mystical power flowing between the two fingers--God's and Adam's--it brings to mind the almost palpable magic that exists between the storyteller and the listener. If it were possible to measure this force as scientists measure electrical current, the charge would be found to consist of attitudes, lifestyles, and le conte. When the voltage is strong enough, one finds the current carrying also the meanings of listening, manners, methods, persons, and purposes. A consideration of the first ingredients, however, is enough to start a study.

The good storyteller is one who has spent years reading, participating in the arts, and, knowingly or unknowingly, preparing to share literature with others. One discovers that enjoying stories alone is not enough, and eventually that there is little pleasure in spending endless hours amusing oneself alone. True enjoyment is a joint endeavor, and one must be prepared to be worthy of receptive ears. The potential storyteller, as the apprentice teacher, senses that one learns to do by doing.

The storyteller accepts that it is unfair to experiment with one's listeners, and that one must not insist on their suffering ineptitude. Personal pride and sensitive planning will be supportive to the apprentice, preventing even the earliest trials from ending in failure. Respect for one's audience rules out worthless material as well as poor performance, because the storyteller is aware that no ragged presentation of a shoddy tale should be foisted upon a trusting group. The listener, like Adam, should receive a perfect gift.

The teller recognizes the listener as partner not only

7

as a recipient, but also as a source of motivation and
strength.   The good storyteller never denigrates the influences that emanate from a listener.   Accordingly, the audience is welcomed as all-important when the storyteller is
moved by a literary experience and is impatient to share it.

It would be fortunate indeed, when one wishes to experiment with new stories, new techniques, or a new group,
that experienced and empathetic listeners are available.   When
the apprentice can elicit the constructive help of such an assembly and place the listeners at ease as co-experimenters,
the reciprocal experience is rich.   As winners or losers, the
group is delighted to be involved; eager to share the outcome
whatever it may be.

When one is not so lucky, the storyteller must be
ready to ask frankly for the listeners' help.   One storyteller
often uses such a procedure when telling stories to a group
for the first time, or when she is experimenting with sophisticated material.   Such a foray is part of the learning process,
and the storyteller generally finds sympathetic people practically impatient to be a part of something exploratory.   She
is met with refreshing courtesy and unbelievable enthusiasm
and, when the program is concluded, the stories are pro-
nounced to be "the very best butter."

Setting such a mood, however, is easy when one is
experienced (and no unforeseen difficulties arise).   Then, one
moves smoothly into the story, relaxed and reassured; finish-
ing the story with poise and grace, secure in the knowledge
that rapport with one's audience is more greatly to be desired than faerie gold.   An apprentice in the art will assess
early the need for the power to arouse empathy within prospective listeners, and will do well to communicate an honest
desire to give pleasure, to make new friends, to be one with
these listening companions.   This happy attitude may be the
only introduction needed in presenting oneself to an audience.
The bearing of the teller--presence, dress, body movements
--all speak volumes before the tale is begun, and a simple
setting-forth of the characters and the scenery against which
they will move is enough to convince the group that cozy fun
is in store--and festival reigns.

Good experiences that help to build total awareness of
one's prospective audiences are gathered through observation
and listening to others.   Once, a storyteller who was speaking with a man in an office supply store about typing paper

and file cards suddenly realized he was anxious to tell her of
a happening that had touched him deeply. The man poured
out a modern version of the folktale theme that gold brings
death.

Of Oriental origin, the first instance of its use is
found in the Jataka tales. [1] Chaucer[2] and Kipling[3] have written on this theme, but on a sultry August day it was repeated
once again with all the traditional innuendoes. The narrator
apparently was unaware of its heritage and of the fascination
it had for his listener. The clerk finished his tale, and completed the sales slip for some inconsequential sum, probably
unaware of the invaluable gift he had shared. The storyteller
must first be a listener; awareness of others' stories shapes
and nourishes the art.

The reading of books about and for all kinds of chil-
dren--Sue Ellen,[4] The Cat and the Coffee Drinkers,[5] The
Lonesome Boy,[6] And the Waters Prevailed,[7] Shadrach,[8] and
The Secret River[9]--opens whole new aspects of childhood to
those who have forgotten, honing the edge of understanding.
Paul Hazard's Books, Children and Men and the works of
Robert Coles should be read and pondered.

Viewing of films about children, too, can soften even
the hardest hearts and sharpen the dullest feelings. Several
that stimulate greater understanding of childhood are "Hello,
Up There," "Reach Out," and "Hopscotch."[10]

The need for a firm background, rooted in literature
and music, comes second only to the immeasurable importance of attitude. Much is written about these two ingredients,
background and attitude, and when one can be confident that
they are possessed, in quantity, it is a comfortable sensation.
The concerned questioner, however, has every right to inquire just what kinds of books, what kinds of music lay the
foundation for a storyteller's success. Can an overwhelming
desire to tell stories balance with a sketchy or belatedly ac-
quired formal approach to the storyteller's art? Can a late
but strong motivation to learn a new skill make up for bar-
ren years?

One morning in a country shack in the South, a young
black woman announced she was ready to tell stories. The
group assembled was the following of a media mini-bus that
made stops around the community, staying in one area only
long enough to offer books and materials, and to allow for

one or two short stories. On this day about fifteen boys and
girls of assorted ages (and three ethnic backgrounds) sat down
at once, clapped their hands, and commanded that the stories
begin.

In clear, soft, too-often ridiculed speech--dropping
endings, "mispronouncing" some words--she repeated stories
she had heard from the van staff during the summer: tales
from the Appalachians, fairy tales from Ireland, and the
texts of contemporary picture books. No tale offered by the
staff had ever come from such a loving heart--was ever before told by a sweeter tongue. The boys and girls, and the
staff, were mesmerized, and they made the stories their own
for always.

Every week, in a neighboring county, a radio station
broadcast a sophisticated program of folktales set off by appropriate music for purposes of background, pauses, and emphasis. The most unbelievable ingredient of the presentations,
however, was the seemingly effortless performances of voice-
changes, impersonations, and mimicry. Too, there was perfect timing and alluring announcements of materials to be borrowed from the county library. The young star was just
seventeen, a graduate of the local county high school, and
for six months she had been serving as an assistant in the
children's room of the main library facility. She came from
a family that had had few advantages; she certainly had heard
few storytellers. Later, when she participated in a storytellers' clinic, she was an amazement to the professionals
present. Her background in reading, sparse; in music, recordings of the 1960's.

From a small class in storytelling, one student told
the story of "The Peddler and His Caps"[11] at a tell-in, and
duplicated the perfect understated and lazy humor with which
it is written. Another from the class brought new life to
"The Blind Men and the Elephant,"[12] and a third breathed
vigor into "The Three Sillies,"[13] after so many years of its
being told both poorly and well. Although each of these three
students held at least one degree from an accredited university, their résumés showed little evidence of the study and
experiences needed for the production of such perfect cameo
performances.

The enrichment that had been missing was exactly what
each was seeking: they wanted to create a working background
--they wanted to learn to tell stories. Hence, they had come

to school to learn to do just that. An impressive background
is an asset, of course, but industry and determination are
not to be denied.

The one source that has smoothed the path for most
contemporary storytellers is Ruth Sawyer's magnificent The
Way of the Storyteller. To this sensitive and wise volume
storytellers turn for information, practical help, inspiration,
and superb tales. It helps to build a sturdy foundation for
any teller of tales. It is enlightening and stimulating for the
inexperienced; it is the old friend and considerate adviser to
the professional. A second reading of Sawyer works sheer
magic in reawakening those who have begun to think other
media have taken the place of the live storyteller as solid
entertainment for today's youth.

Listening to music, to stories, to plays, to people
speaking; reading the folktales and short stories of yesterday
and today; studying the folklorists who have searched among
literature and discovered new aspects of the old tales; haunt-
ing reference sources that reconfirm one's belief that a shared
story experience is a superior way to entertain (and a teaching technique not to be despised): these are the building materials needed for the development of the storyteller--but they
can be gathered as one goes along.

Although one must be cognizant of the immediate audience to please, when storytellers go about searching for acceptable material they need not be concerned only with a current engagement. When one reads and likes a selection,
wherever it may be, a note of the location should be made
and kept available. A tale-teller's finding le conte that measures up is like a Forty-Niner's finding gold. Reading Sawyer,
one finds "The Magic Box"[14]; Shedlock, "To Your Good
Health."[15] While these may not be the first stories an apprentice should choose, they should be noted and read, and
sneezing is such an opportunity for a storyteller![16]

Hidden away in Kate Douglas Wiggin's Tales of Laughter is "Jack and the King Who Was a Jintleman" (in some
collections with a more prosaic spelling). Many of the old
tales have been saved when their original sources have gone
out of print, but it is a loss that more of the stories of robust good humor have not been preserved. One is the poorer
when the older titles no longer remain on lists or in catalogs.

Charlotte Krum's Four Riders has delighted too many

children to be omitted from prominent listings.   "Talk"[17]
has first been discovered, by some not familiar with Courlander, in a film on storytelling.[18]   The delicate "Golden
Cobwebs" and the amusing "Jimmy Scarecrow's Christmas"
are tucked away in The Children's Book of Christmas Stories.[19]

     Finding the perfect story for a difficult assignment
could take days of searching, but during this time one turns
up several excellent selections for use later.   How convenient
it is to find in one's files, titles and sources for such as
"The Devil and Daniel Webster,"[20] "The Holy Lake,"[21] "The
Open Window,"[22] "The Magic Shop,"[23] and the scores of magnificent short stories relished by young adults.

     It is frustrating to discover that many educators be-
lieve storytelling is primarily for the young child.   Why, then,
is it true that so great a number of them have never heard
of the old nursery favorites?   They have never heard them
told or read.

     Nevertheless, unless one has a large personal library,
or has access to an adequate collection, it is hard to find
good stories for all ages.   The situation grows even more
critical when the storyteller does not have a broad background
in literature.   In any case, a personal, available list is necessary and convenient.

     In searching for the right story for the occasion at
hand, the storyteller will have already considered the potential audience.   Sometimes it is not easy to convince some
planners that a particular program, if it happens to fall within a holiday period, does not have to include seasonal stories.   With a few exceptions, of course--for instance, special
requests for material appropriate to certain holy days--any
good story will be better than a mediocre tale reiterating the
beauties of spring, the crisp air of autumn; the capers of
Saint Nicholas.   Ghost stories do not have to be saved for
Halloween.

     Tales of the macabre are acceptable to almost any
audience and so far as young children are concerned it is
not necessary to withhold tales of ordinary violence and re-
ality (they adore them), since the experienced storyteller is
skilled in the art of softening the impact of a near-devastat-
ing sequence.   Here a storyteller shows a true understanding
of the art, since the cushioning process does not come through

a change of words and phrases, but through the voice, the face, and the body. The storyteller accepts and appreciates the force of the tale and its meaning.

One must be courageous in not limiting oneself to stories for specific age groups. Storytelling has never divided itself into levels. Read-aloud story writers write their best for themselves; they sometimes are not concerned with the ages of their readers or listeners. They wish merely that their works be read and be told.

It is fallacious to believe that young children cannot be entertained by stories to which older boys and girls relate; that elementary students cannot be held with selections used with young adults and grown-ups.

For hundreds of years children everywhere have selected from among adult literature what they liked best. They have made it their own. Military personnel, Rotarians, and Kiwanians have been delighted with "Master of All Masters," "Teeny Tiny," "Molly Whuppie," and "Whittington and His Cat."[24] "Schnitzle, Schnotzle, and Schnootzle,"[25] has held all-male adult groups; "The Poor Count's Christmas,"[26] large congregations. Ten-year-olds, boards of trustees, and deacons have been enthralled by "The Devil...."[27]

The story hour, too often replaced with an entertainment carefully programmed for the very young, seldom attracts the little leaguers. Indeed, they may not be welcome. This type of program will not hold even the very young, in the future. Children have been exposed to all of life's tragedies and joys whether or not they have found pleasure in them, or have understood them. It must not be overlooked that even the three- and four-year-olds have had to help care for infants at home. They have watched good television drama (though with the continuity broken by dozens of commercials) and kept some sense of story. They have spent hours drawing and painting, cutting paper-dolls, and supervising the family shopping at the supermarket.

Educators have been too quick in saying that the interest span of children is short. A child's interest span is just that: an interest span! Doesn't one hear a muted call for help? So long as an object, a subject, an activity--a person--can hold their attention, children will listen, work, play, or "pretend" until they are physically exhausted (or until they are very, very hungry!). When the overriding con-

cern of some planners of children's programs is, in truth,
to allow parents to get away for an adult attack on the supermarket, an assault on the gasoline pump, or for an opportunity to collect another member of the household from music
or dancing lessons, it is nigh impossible to convince children
of their own importance.

Why not plan a story program of listening--for children? All comers will be welcome.

Indisputably, the story hour has suffered a sea change.
With the finger-plays and song breaks came the name tags,
the schedules, the maximum safe numbers to be accommodated
in tiny rooms, the signing-up, the exclusion of parents....
The real story hour, like Tom Tit Tot, may have given "an
awful shriek and away that flew into the dark."[28] Too, the
real nightingale may have flown "out of the open window back
into its green woods."[29]

NOTES

1. Chaucer, ed. Robinson: p. 834.

2. Ibid.: "The Pardoner's Tale," pp. 181-187.

3. Kipling, Jungle Books: "The King's Ankus,"
pp. 123-148.

4. Hunter.

5. Steele.

6. Bontemps.

7. Barringer.

8. DeJong.

9. Rawlings.

10. See under their titles in the FILM part of the
Bibliography.

11. Tooze: pp. 81-83; no credits listed as to source.

12. Quigley.

13. Jacobs: pp. 10-15.

14. Sawyer: pp. 219-225.

15. Shedlock: pp. 183-90.

16. Ibid.

17. Courlander and Herzog: pp. 25-29.

18. "Art of Telling Stories...."

19. Dickinson and Skinner: Sara Cone Bryant, pp. 193-195, and Mary E. Wilkins Freeman, pp. 103-112.

20. Benét

21. Sawyer, Long Christmas: pp. 123-133.

22. Saki: pp. 288-291.

23. Isherwood: H. G. Wells, pp. 156-171.

24. Jacobs: pp. 230-231; 57-58; 130-135; 174-185.

25. Sawyer, Long Christmas: pp. 69-81.

26. Harper: Frank R. Stockton, pp. 44-54.

27. Benét.

28. Jacobs: p. 9.

29. Shedlock: p. 251.

Chapter Three

THE HALL--AND ALL

Bracketed against the stone walls, the torches flamed
golden red, scattering the shadows in the great hall of the
castle, four-towered and grey against the night sky.   Seated
at oaken tables men and women ate and drank.   Fires added
to the light of the flares; the smell of roasting meat filled
the space.   Dogs and children played on skins upon the floor.

It was evening, and a minstrel in flowing blue and
green cape stood near the central hearth.   As deep as the
odor of the browning meat was the hush of the family and
its guests.   Their eagerness was as bright as the fires; anticipation, as sweet as the wine.   He would bring news of the
lands beyond the castle, of battles and storm; of gods, evil
and good; of men and of stars.   It was story time.

It is understandable why children thrill to the Middle
Ages; why anyone will sit and listen when a storyteller begins
a tale of that time.   Since there are few castles to come by,
and fewer troubadors, there must be careful planning to rep-
licate the excitement and grandeur of the medieval scene.

Comfort, with a sense of space, light, and warmth,
must pervade even the smallest cubby--wherever stories are
to be told.   The surroundings should be carefully controlled
to make sure the speaker may present a meaningful, happy
sharing; an occasion that can blossom into a moving experience.   And the time to set this special moment is before:
before a story is selected, before it is learned, before one
hangs out the posters and the signs, or lights the candle
commemorating the ancient castle flares and hearth.   To
guide the planning, one may summon up Kipling's six serving
men: Why, Who, When, Where, What, and How. [1] "Why"
is purpose: always entertainment.

Sometimes it is possible to combine entertainment with

16

incidental teaching, the approach being a simple introduction
of honorable women and men who have changed history: Jane
Addams, Magdalena Bach, Madame Marie Curie, Benjamin
Franklin, Saskia van Rijn, George Washington, and a thousand more.

One storyteller confided that it was one of her greatest
pleasures to say: "May I present General George Washington?" to a group of jaded junior high students who had been
quoted as having said that they hated "G. Washington, who
hung on every classroom wall: stoney-eyed, bewigged--a
real klutz. ..." She said she always grew excited when she
told of Washington and Franklin on their way to Philadelphia
discussing thoughtfully the sturdy, brilliant, upstart patriot
who was causing so much trouble in Boston, Paul Revere.

It must be thought through carefully, this purpose,
lest the program be a genuine time-waster, a filler, a replacement for a story experience.   No presentation should
ever be allowed to dissolve into a spur-of-the-moment crutch;
it must never be a weaker part of an event.   This is not
storytelling.   Neither is it an occasion for reward, nor should
story hours be planned just because there is to be a holiday.
To implement the true purpose, the storyteller must be in
charge of the planning, or be asked, if a guest, to supervise
the segment to be conducted by the storyteller.   When the
guest agrees to accept a request presentation, it is wise to
inquire into the matter of "Why," as well as to "When" and
"Where."   There are times when stories may be spontaneous,
but these should be rare.

When one is invited to dinner where there are young
children, almost always, if it is known that the guest is a
storyteller, the hosts offer indulgently an opportunity for the
storyteller to tell a tale during the evening to the children;
sometimes to the group as a whole.   The well-meaning hosts
may suggest that the teller take the children into the family
room, or, they may specify such a time when the children
are to say goodnight.   But these situations are easy to control: the storyteller says either yes or no, making good on
the decision.

Now and again one may be called upon to bemuse (in
the old meaning of the word) a group of youngsters at or just
after a time of crisis, or during a storm, or to moderate
personnel problems in a school, or to substitute, on a moment's notice, for a canceled program of another type.   It

is well to have firm policies governing such emergencies.
A poorly-told story (because of no chance for freshening of
material) will not succeed in calming overly-stimulated boys
and girls, or senior citizens who have just witnessed the
burning of their rest home.

Meeting such emergencies, of course, lies within the
judgment of the storyteller. In less threatening crises, one
may call upon one's repertoire for an old favorite that has
been shared so often brushing up may not be necessary.
There does arise the screamingly amusing but personally
miserable situation of having been misinformed concerning
a special assignment, causing the whole program to disinte-
grate. Even the best laid plans can go awry. Perhaps the
most humorous tales a storyteller could ever tell would be
the accounts of her or his own experiences with situations
of this nature.

Once a very confident storyteller accepted an invitation to demonstrate story-hour procedures before a large and
not overly sympathetic audience. Children had been invited
to come to form a nucleus of listeners and to be observed:
their degree of attention to denote the value of storytelling;
the expertise of the storyteller. The group was to have consisted of third, fourth, and fifth graders, but when the children marched in, it was apparent that some mistake had been
made. The boys and girls were bright-eyed, rambunctious
three-, four-, and five-year-olds and on holiday yet! "So
cute ... just the right age ... (sometimes thought to be the
only age) ... to be interested in stories...," went the whispered comments. The moment hung dark as rainy midnight,
but nothing loath the storyteller, quickly changing material,
stuck it like a true professional. It was evident, however,
at the close of the meeting that the presentation had been
less than a ringing success.

On another occasion, a small group of boys and girls,
touched by some wicked magician's wand, turned into nearly
three hundred citizens of assorted ages; looking for free food
and something to do on a holiday in a small town. As if that
were not enough, here came a life-sized (human) pink-and-
white rabbit to play peek-a-boo with the storyteller.

Confusion reigned once for a storyteller when ten-
year-olds grew into bus-loads of rough and ready young males
(presumably tenth-graders) from a large country high school.
Selections from Robert A. Heinlein's Citizen of the Galaxy

pulled the chestnuts from the fire. So, one should elicit as
much information as possible about planned programs and not
only for self-defense: material presented in such events should
reflect the particular interests and needs of the audience.
The guest storyteller should be brave and ask questions.

One should inquire the "why" of the occasion. Since
stories may be desired for any number of different audiences,
it is well to know if the event is to celebrate a holiday, or
if it is to mark a special observance; whether or not the appearance is to be for a literary group, a children's party,
or for a gathering of golden-agers. Is the group a civic club?
Is it a woman's club, a social gathering of the sewing circle?
Often storytellers are invited to come as a break in a regular
series of programs planned for travel clubs, book clubs, and
sorority meetings. Grandmothers as well as new mothers get
the wind up, as the English are proported to say, over good
books and reading stories to children, and their combined
conscience calls for an authority to come and set them straight.
A storyteller is often considered the pleasantest way for all
this to be resolved. The storyteller should also know when
on a certain program the story may be scheduled.

Similarly, a program chairperson may invite a well-
known writer of children's books to appear as the main
speaker or storyteller for a convention banquet. It is well
for such a writer to ask "why" a story is being chosen for
a part of the program instead of special music, a jokester,
or a news commentator. The answer will shed much light.
When it is known "why," the guest may be able to judge
whether or not to accept the invitation.

The experienced storyteller may discount these instructions for cautionary measures, but apprentices should not
place themselves in any situation where they may find the
waters too deep. The storyteller should always be prepared
for all emergencies and interruptions, but to know early on
some of the problems that may arise is to be able to start
in the right direction.

When the program chairperson is communicative about
the event to come, the guest should continue and ask "when"
and "where" the story will be told, the length of time allotted, and, if the storyteller wishes, the age-range of the audience. Stories should be for all comers, but being informed
about what one can expect is helpful and will, of course, influence selection.

Many similar questions may also be put and when the answers are satisfactory the storyteller may accept the invitation and complete the arrangements. If the occasion is a repeat performance to a familiar group, there is little need to question carefully. Then, the storyteller will want to consult any notes and files that may have been made regarding that previous appearance. One should find there information stating the success of the earlier program, the stories told, and, if it were a television presentation, what was worn.

Although one may think this information would be offered spontaneously by the host, especially "when" and "where," such is not always the case. It is much less startling when one knows in advance that the stories will be told next to a playground, near a room being utilized by the high school marching band, or if the story hour is to take place on a trail leading to the motorcycle track.

When a storyteller is to play host, one should remember one's own experiences, sad or glad, and hasten to enlighten any guest. The "resident" storyteller should extend special courtesy: be present to introduce the guest and to listen to the program, unless the guest knows in advance that the host will not be present, and why, and that certain substitutions will be necessary.

The ideal situation is when the storyteller is also the program planner. But regardless who tells, plans, or is in charge, no one is more important than the audience itself.

The ancient storytellers did not have to be concerned with arrangements. They knew whom to expect: women, men, children, dogs, horses, slaves--in short, the whole community. They had to please the man who furnished the supper and the place for sleeping, and it was the news they brought--and the freshness of the tale--that was of significance. They also had been trained by masters of the art, or of their guilds: it is only recently that most storytellers have had to go it on their own.

Some think it doesn't take much to gather a group of children on a break from their nursery school, or a class waiting to go to lunch. The time is overdue, however, when all storytellers should accept the degree of sophistication of even a small gathering of quite young children. Notice should be taken of the listening experience of boys and girls, especially including their handicaps, language barriers, and whe- or not they can hear at all!

When the storyteller is also in charge of planning, and if time, space, staff, and money are available, one must decide who in the community would benefit most from hearing stories. However pleasant and simple it may be to welcome into a public library a small group of well-dressed, privileged youngsters from an exclusive kindergarten, taking a program to an inner-city school or playground may be the real mission.

Organizing listening experiences for the older elementary school students presents problems, but to no other group is a storyteller more welcome, especially when one comes first as a friend. It is only too true that these are the kids who have been neglected. Controls of story programs in the past few years have limited the numbers of listeners and have put in place so many rules and restrictions that they have not been able to be met by teachers and parents in certain communities. It takes a well-organized household to remember to sign up for a story program at the right time, to keep a calendar of changing dates and hours. In addition, now that yesterday's very young have "grown up" to be so busy and so loud, administrators can be slow to invite them.

It was to expiate these concerns that such a thing as registration was initiated; but this discourages those who quail before formality. Another problem arises when young visitors are accompanied by adults. Some parents prefer to remain with their children, but this possible intrusion can have alarming ramifications. Is the storyteller afraid of adults? (Woe be to the narrator whose presentation is no better than second class.) Do adults really cause enough trouble to warrant their being excluded? It should be for the storyteller to decide, though sometimes it is not left to his or her choice.

The most exciting of all program planning is arranging for a series of story hours for inexperienced listeners in an attempt to addict them to the need for hearing stories in a group.

An instructor in storytelling has been quoted as saying to a student, who reported difficult experiences with youngsters in a large central-city area, that in the future the location would be dropped from the schedule. If true, this decision is a sad commentary on the philosophy of a professional storyteller-instructor. Of all groups who should be encouraged to learn to listen, to have multiple opportunities to hear stories, inner-city children present the greatest challenge. The instructor would have been short-sighted, to say

the least, since it is through this kind of situation that apprentices may learn to refine their skills to be able to reach
the most difficult of audiences. Perhaps a change of storytellers would have been a better remedial action. More training and an improvement in technique for and by the same student would have been ideal. This type of group teaches the
storyteller more than an instructor who stands, or too often
sits, in a classroom and lectures.

        Audiences should not be sought just to be used as
targets for teller exposure. The storyteller, even the apprentice, should wish to master the art as far as possible
before making a presentation. Artists draw, compose, write,
tell a story first for their own pleasure, and second for the
pleasure of sharing. Seeking an audience previous to having
something to give is the mark of an enthusiastic experimenter
and amateur. The beginning storyteller should also learn to
choose among available opportunities those from which both
speaker and listener may profit most.

        Two additional components of the planning procedure
are "when" and "where." "When" the program is to take
place often delimits "where" or not "where." "Where" often
spells out "when." Scheduling and location interact since requests for storytellers may come from long or short distances. The community for which a storyteller is responsible for planning story hours may be large, and distances
between locations may be restrictive. "When" also denotes
length of program as well as that part of a week or hour of
the day it is to be set. "When" also must be translated to
give meaning to the most convenient hour for a particular
community to be free to attend. Here again, the prospective
audience should be allowed to govern both location and time
of day or night. It is from within this framework that the
planner must proceed.

        After these problems have been carefully studied and
resolved, and "when" and "where" have been established, let
nothing interfere with these choices. Regularity will serve
the planner well, and the public has a right to know securely
in advance.

        The size of the potential group will dictate "where"
since uncrowded audiences are much more comfortable, more
ready to listen, and more eager to be actively involved. The
mobility of most audiences is not so limitless as may be
thought. A storyteller must be ready to take the mountain to

Mahomet--or the other way around.   Often the "where" is
forced, but the "when" should demonstrate a reason.

   Storytelling may be practiced in almost any spot.   A
one-to-one relationship between a storyteller and a child who
is in a bathtub can be as rewarding as a presentation before
a thousand senior-high-school students in an immense gymnas-
ium.   It is thrilling to recall such a group listening to a
shortened version of Bishop's Pancakes--Paris, but no more
so than "Teeny Tiny" in a tub!

   The first rule to remember when choosing the location
is that the expected audience be allowed enough space, with
room for wheelchairs, to sit, lounge, and to react bodily,
in as attractive an area as can be arranged.   A too-popular
place should not be chosen if such a selection means that the
listeners may be hurrrrrrried at the conclusion of the stories.   A full listing of locations for children's programs is
given on page 3 of Bauer's Handbook for Storytellers.

   The "what" and the "how" of the occasion are almost
as interchangeable as the "when" and "where."   In reaching
for the elegance of simplicity, the storyteller may forget all
the mechanics of a starched-up affair and resort to just telling the story.   What shall be chosen?   Should there be more
than one story?   Would the program be more effective with
music?   With poetry?   With an intermission?   Should the
material be more visually oriented?   Is there time enough
to search for the perfect story?

   There are occasions when the prepared program just
doesn't seem to fit an audience, and the wise storyteller will
have prepared more material than may be needed.   Wasn't
it Maria Edgeworth, the didactic English writer who, after
her experiences with seventeen younger brothers and sisters,
suggested that one have two strings for one's bow?[2]   Arbuthnot says there were twenty younger brothers and sisters![3]

   When a storyteller is training young children to be
listeners it is sometimes necessary to have support from a
second medium.   One speaker working with a batch of three-
year-olds found that they enjoyed a story more after they had
seen it first on a filmstrip.   After a rather slow beginning
with the story, the Weston Woods filmstrip of The Biggest
Bear[4] caught their attention and helped the youngsters to have
some acquaintance with Johnny Orchard.   Later, the same
morning, the storyteller told the story with pleasure all a-

round. One wonders what her experiences had been that enabled her to figure out this technique.

Thus, the listener not only influences the selection of material but also the manner of presentation. It is best to be prepared.

The sophisticated short stories of John O'Hara, Isak Dinesen, Conrad Aiken, and John Updike would please a totally different audience from that which would find pleasure in "The Three Sillies" and "Jack and the Beanstalk," or tales from Andersen or Wilde. The storyteller will learn, however, that any audience of children will be pleased with most modern tales of original themes and the full-bodied folktales from the collections of Jacobs and from the many excellent compilations by Virginia Haviland.

Proper planning seems endless, but the task need not be arduous. Using the same technique so valuable in learning a story--allowing the total picture of the program to run through the mind--the planner-storyteller can see the presentation in its entirety. The whole event will be visible from the moment of inception through publicity, to the color and taste of the edible (sometimes) favors. Other embellishments of the program may consist of story-hour symbols: a candle, a bell, or a story-hour banner. Fresh flowers, a collection of books for borrowing after the stories, or a special time set aside for looking at pictures or picture books after the program may be added.

Attractive garments (but seldom outright costumes) for the storyteller, and proper arrangements for the cleaning and decorating of the story area will round out plans and assure the planner that all is in order; that the event will bring fun and meaning.

Whether or not favors are distributed, whether or not food is to be served, or offered for taking home, will be governed by the character of the program, good taste, and the various local policies controlling eating in public buildings, funds for such extensions for this type of affair, and the size of the staff. There is, of course, a certain charm afforded through the provision of such extras.

At the conclusion of a carefully-planned program on an explanation of the five senses, during a story hour of the PLACE project at the Forsyth County Public Library, in Win-

ston-Salem, North Carolina, small paper napkin pokes of pop-
corn were given to the children. Stories in keeping with the
theme, activities including helping pop the corn (smelling the
delicious procedure, listening to the bursting kernels) would
have meant far less if the product itself could not have been
shared! It just had to be tasted.

A spur-of-the-moment story experience, when the
storyteller gathers several children together on a rainy afternoon, is rewarding for both adult and children, but when
storytellers wish to expand their audiences, to reach more
ears and hearts and minds, they should learn to hone their
skills and to structure entertainment worthy of the art.

NOTES

1. Kipling, ed. Beecroft: pp. 383-384; a tailpiece
to "The Elephant's Child," "I keep six honest serving men. . . . "

2. Gardner and Ramsey: p. 175.

3. Arbuthnot, Children. . . : p. 21.

4. Ward.

Chapter Four

A TALE TO TELL

Whole books, like shoes, must fit; but stories being more elastic may be compared with hosiery and gloves. Listeners cannot be so easily "fitted up" with stories as they are umbrellas or purses, but shopping for the right story is more pleasure than work.

Supermarkets spread their wares to be seen, but a shoe store has always been a mystery. The clerk bobs back into the depths of a cavern, and returns long after bringing boxes with markings as unintelligible as the Latin on a doctor's prescription slip. Some large library collections are housed as shoes are, but it is fun to browse from shelf to shelf when permitted.

How easy it would be to have keys to help locate the "right" story. Trees may be identified through keys to the generic groups; after checking general shape, fruit, leaves and stipules, a tree outdoors may be matched to one in a book.

There are similar keys for the identification of birds. One begins with size, moves to color, to wing bars. If it is necessary to go further, the color of the beak or peculiarity of tufting or whiskering (as with the whippoorwill) may lead to the naming of a particular bird. (The long bristles of the whippoorwill do the watcher little good since the whippoorwill is wary of the day, flying only at night. When safely hidden these birds plague lazy sleepers with their naughty admonitions.)

Dr. Wilburt C. Davison, noted pediatrician and first dean of the Duke University Medical School, in his 1934 The Compleat Pediatrician, arranged another kind of guide: lists of symptoms by which the diseases of children can be verified. A physician may rule out--or in--fever, rashes, swellings and with this help can make a tentative diagnosis.

If the storyteller is confused by keys and guides, perhaps it would be helpful if one could feed into a computer various components and receive a print-out list of stories. The computer could be instructed that a story for a large, mixed group of youngsters was wanted; that it should be long enough to last fifteen or twenty minutes. By touching other buttons the storyteller could pull out a printed list including "Molly Whuppie,"[1] "The Elephant's Child,"[2] "The Hungry Old Witch,"[3] "How Boots Befooled the King,"[4] "The Princess Whom Nobody Could Silence,"[5] and The Five Hundred Hats of Bartholomew Cubbins. [6]

It would also be necessary to know in which collections the stories were to be found, and what libraries owned copies of these collections. The question of availability would have to be dealt with by the searcher. However, until there are keys and guides and computers to provide this service, modern minstrels must rely on their background of tales known for stories they would like to present.

A firm background in reading, courses in literature, and work in bookstores and libraries puts one far along in the search. The librarian is familiar with arrangement systems, with collections of stories, indexes, and the authors and titles of full-length books that have lively chapters to be lifted out for sharing. Visits to card catalogs and to story collections will supply the information one needs concerning a library's holdings of folklore and fairy tales. A glance at Index to Fairy Tales ... [7] will show several versions of the most popular stories and in what books they are to be found, but the storyteller has to obtain the story and read it before choosing or rejecting.

One may not assume that storytellers have access to unlimited material. Many libraries have small collections, and often libraries needing the most in basic holdings have in fact the fewest stories. If one eschews the computer approach and is working only with the titles of favorite stories, one may soon discover that the nearest library facility cannot supply the desired volume. Small libraries (with even smaller budgets) may be willing to spend a certain amount for a beginning collection of material, but the number of good, tellable stories per collection is often limited. Some anthology titles offer higher percentages of acceptable stories than others,

but small libraries cannot hire bibliographers or acquisition-
ers who would be familiar with them.

The storyteller meets another obstacle in poorly-
stocked libraries: the paucity of good reference tools that
could help to locate materials to be procured through inter-
library loan. The frustration grows since in communities
where library facilities are meager, storytelling is often
needed most. The apprentice may settle for a newly published picture book and prepare puppets or flannel boards constructed with materials available in shopping centers.

The earnest storyteller, however, is like the fox in
search of someone to sew back his tail,[8] and goes from lists,
to catalogs, from bibliographies to publishers' promotional
material, and to reviews. The need for keeping a list (and
a copy of a good story) begins to emerge, and the student
does well to heed this warning. One lecturer on storytelling
always begins by saying, "If I were ever stranded with children on a desert island, I'd want to have a copy of Jacobs
in my pocket!" Another good collection (if one has time to
prepare for that desert island) is Gruenberg's Favorite Stories Old and New. Two other compilations contain a high per-
centage of tellable stories: Giants and Witches and a Dragon
or Two and Princesses and Peasant Boys, both by Phyllis R.
Fenner.

Even when an acceptable story is actually in hand, the
storyteller may discover that this material is covered by
copyright regulations that restrict its use. It is well to seek
permission from the publisher, especially if the material is
to be used on radio or television. Even librarians and offi-
cials of radio and television companies are not always knowledgeable of what printed material may be used. Some storytellers may remember that years ago it was almost impossible to secure permission for broadcasting any of Kipling's
stories. Publishers holding copyrights are generous when
they can be, but sometimes fees must be paid. Shedlock
found that the restrictions governing copyrighted material
early in the twentieth century (when laws were less stringent
than they are today) prevented her from making available (in
her writings) many stories she considered good for narration.

For all the hindrances the storyteller has to encounter,
perhaps the one most often experienced, however, is not knowing where to look. This inconvenience is partially removed
by a trip to the public library or to the school media center.

Formal courses in children's literature and in storytelling
also ease this hardship. A true giant step forward was taken
in North Carolina years ago when the state decreed that each
teacher preparing to work with the elementary grades should
receive training in children's literature.

These courses, however, were not always taught by
instructors who were thoroughly acquainted with the subject.
Many had little knowledge of books--or children--and few were
experienced storytellers. Much of what they knew was from
their reading, remembered from their childhoods. This situation precluded the introduction to students of the hundreds
of books published for children in the 1930's and 1940's, as
well as the overwhelming number of titles that have followed
in the next three decades.

The publication explosion in the 1950's and 1960's was
triggered, in part, by the availability of large amounts of
federal funds, and the necessity for schools and public libraries to encumber certain monies from the National Defense
Education Act, the Elementary and Secondary Education Act,
and the Library Services and Construction Act. Additional
problems arose when the instructors discovered that teacher-
training institutions were not eager to share minuscule budgets with a course bearing the ignominious nickname of "Kiddie Lit."

Library schools have offered excellent courses in children's and young adult literature and in non-print materials,
but there were few separate classes in storytelling taught in
the 1950's and 1960's. This subject was generally taught as
a part of the courses on books and materials.

Many students who are required to study children's
and young adults' literature at both the undergraduate and
graduate levels are often those very students who receive this
instruction in evening and extension courses. Too, they have
little time for the amounts of reading necessary to lay a firm
background for selection. Wide reading is unavoidable if one
wishes to know where the mines of superior stories are.

This welter of trouble for the storyteller is softened
through help by primary selectors and critics who prune the
field. Reviews of story collections and annotated lists make
the job easier. Ruth Tooze, who was a teacher, storyteller,
traveler, writer, and critic, put many helpful pages in her
Storytelling. A balance of the old and new in material (to

1959) is found here, and the author has grouped materials
loosely enough to aid speakers looking for something for large,
mixed audiences. Lists and collections prepared by storytellers are of greater value than those that present material
for other purposes and are often arranged according to form
or subject.

Other excellent sources for lists of good stories to
tell are found in publications of the New York Public Library,
the Carnegie Library of Pittsburgh, and the Enoch Pratt Free
Library. Baker and Greene in their Storytelling: Art and
Technique have added immeasurably to choices for the storyteller.

For the uninitiated, the selection of a good story presents another quandary. It must be decided just what makes
a story difficult to prepare, and how diligent an apprentice
is willing to work since many of the most appealing tales appear to be the most difficult. When the teller is familiar
with a story, however involved it may seem to others, preparation time is shortened. Much of "The Elephant's Child,"[9]
"How They Broke Away to Go to the Rootabaga Country,"[10]
and The Bojabi Tree[11] must be so well remembered that none
of the exquisite flavor is lost. The learning of these stories
could be equivalent to memorization. To experience the sharing of these particular stories, however, is more than worth
the effort.

Beginners may be discouraged from preparing tales
such as these, but an instructor should never interfere when
a student is determined to try. The challenge to prove an
instructor in error is great, and the apprentice will generally
do a good job. Too, there is something to be said for allowing (or even requesting) students in a controlled group, where
they have instructional aid, to start with a demanding selection.

An instructor experimenting with selection and degrees
of difficulty, asked each of a group of students to learn the
same story, The Five Chinese Brothers.[12] The story is not
excessively long; there are familiar patterns; but there are
areas which must be treated with care. After three days
members of the group told the story to each other in class,
with nervousness noted in only two of the first-timers. Out
of a class of ten, only two had had any previous storytelling
experience; the selection had been made for them, and the
learning of it had been done by their own methods before any
classroom discussion of technique.

Comparative information from other storytelling teachers about the advantages of students' beginning a crash course with the learning of one moderately difficult story to save precious time would have been useful. But lacking such information, the project was thoroughly explained, and the cooperation of the class was requested. Demonstrations by the instructor were given starting on the first day, but at no time did she tell the story being used in the exercise. She was, however, an enthusiastic listener.

The students were deeply involved with the study also; two of the eight who had had no previous experience were judged, in secret voting by their classmates, to have given a most creditable performance.

The stumbling block for the others was trying to get straight which brother had what miraculous ability, but at the conclusion of the experiment, it was felt that the students had benefited from starting with a story to learn (instead of a lecture) and that the selection had been a medium-to-hard one to master.

A lengthy discussion of the brothers and their special gifts that followed the learning project pointed up the value of such a step in the preparation process. Before the course was over, the students were laughing about it all and calling themselves "the ten Chinese sisters."

Following the experiment, simple folktales appeared to be a breeze. "The Old Woman and Her Pig," "Teeny Tiny," and "Master of All Masters" were learned rapidly and told well. These three stories[13] are short, but they present special opportunities for innovation. Whether or not the story is easy to learn, the first factor to be considered in selection is the audience with whom it is to be shared. The second most important consideration should be the literary merit of the material.

Many writers of storytelling procedure find it necessary to emphasize the point that the material should be liked before it is chosen. There is some doubt, however, that storytellers ever select a tale they do not enjoy. Doing so would be unfair to all concerned, and few speakers would ever make this mistake.

There is much prejudging--and winnowing out--of stories before final choices are made for telling. Society has already chosen which folktales are to survive, and writers, collectors, and artists have exercised thoughtful care in the preparation of new versions. Editors choose carefully among many manuscripts; the bibliographers and buyers choose what they think will be borrowed or bought.

Too, the opinionated are not in the silent minority. They are quick to let it be known when a certain story may be offensive to a segment of the community. Good taste will prevent the thrusting of a Christmas story upon an audience who had not made a request for such a specific theme. A storyteller will know that many groups prefer "just a good story" unless other choices are made known.

Many stories and books are under clouds, accused of the offences of sexism, national chauvinism, racism. Even The Five Chinese Brothers has become anathema to some. "The Five Chinese Brothers: Time to Retire" is the lead article in a recent issue of Interracial Books for Children Bulletin. [20] What a pity, especially now that the United States Congress is considering extending the age limit for retirement!

Racism--or intolerance of all kind and degree--has robbed children of some attractive stories. But good manners and one's own sensitivity dictate the omission of certain tales when thoughtful folk have judged against them. To Southerners, the hardest story to give up was "The Wonderful Tar-Baby," by Joel Chandler Harris. This story died twice: in one respectable collection it was chopped in half (an omission that may have been due to the compiler's not realizing there was more to it, that the author had used delaying tactics and had finished it up later in the volume in which it had appeared originally). No one could ever just forget Brer Rabbit, "born and bred in a briar patch." The apprentice may wonder if there exists a story anywhere that can pass all tests.

There may be stories that must not be told, but there are those that must be told for it is upon stories that speech, conversation, and advertising are based. References to characters in stories such as these permeate much of living and literature. To fail to recognize the traits, characteristics, habits, and adventures of story friends is never to belong. More practically speaking, the full meanings of news articles and commentaries can sometimes never be appreciated without understanding story characters or actions upon which they may be predicated.

Adult listeners want to be reminded of stories they heard in their youth; to enjoy reliving the robust humor of Mark Twain's "Jim Baker's Bluejay Yarn"[15]; and the under-stated magnificence of "The Piece of String" and "The Diamond Necklace."[16]

Selection of stories for an adult audience can be as time-consuming as choosing tales for youngsters. Older folk like the tales of their childhood, but they are also pleased with stories of strong adventure: characters accomplishing feats that they can no longer perform (or ever could). Tales of the locale in which the listeners live are particularly pop-ular.

The literary quality of a story is more important to an audience that is highly educated, but all adults are willing to listen to simple stories, especially when children are present. Groups of mothers and grandmothers are always eager to hear new stories they can retell later to small kin at nap or bedtime.

When stories are being chosen for a group of quite elderly or handicapped oldsters, several short ones have been found to be better than one long tale. Adult audiences are courteous, but they have a tendency to become restless; to move about even more than small children.

Young adults are easily pleased--believe it or not! Almost any tale worth the telling is well received if it has literary merit and is well told. It should also have that something extra, and the characters should be recreated so well that they act vividly and speak naturally--that they say something worthwhile. A story that moves, has suspense, contains a soupçon of humor, and a conclusion that winds up with a resolution of an earlier identifiable struggle, is most appealing to them.

Folktales contain most of these ingredients. A story-teller was once delighted with a roomful of seniors in a speech class at a prestigious university, who sat in a class-room (one side all glass and open to the busy campus a few steps beyond) and listened to the simplest of cumulative tales.

One snowy afternoon in New York City over thirty years ago, Mary Gould Davis told Seumas MacManus' "Billy Beg and His Bull"[17] to a group of teenage boys en route from one juvenile hall of correction to another. (Somewhere, some-

one cared enough to offer these young men one perfect moment.) With no more ado than to say her name and the title
of her story, she began. Their eyes never left her face:
she mesmerized them completely. She and Billy Beg held
them enthralled.

It is impossible to say what will appeal to young adults
all the time, or any part of the time, and each storyteller
must work the best magic, hoping that the enthusiasm and the
pleasure in the sharing will weld the teller and the listener
together.

On the Saturday morning following the assassination of
President John F. Kennedy, a group of high-school students
at a convention listened to a storyteller tell selections from
the writings of and about this lost and mourned young leader.
Their caring attitude and appreciation of his words alone
seemed almost memorial enough.

The storyteller has a singular obligation in this ques-
tioning age, in that sensitivity and sincerity must accompany
the telling; it is of great importance to be at ease with both
audience and material.

In choosing stories to share with young children, it is
wise to select tales that portray characters doing the things
that small children do.   Children have the ability to relate
to both out-of-doors and inside "sets," and they are comfortable when there is a mixture of adults and children in
the story. This is the type of experience with which young
children are familiar. Humanized animals, too, are pleasing as subjects, and little children do not shy away from fantastic adventures. What have they not imagined all by themselves? Nothing. Relationships, however, must be valid.
It is not necessary that all of the story be easy to understand. Boys and girls know intuitively that mysteries exist
that will unravel themselves when the time comes. They are
willing to accept strange and unfamiliar words. For the most
part, young listeners want a story told by an enthusiastic,
warm person with feeling for the titillating joke, and to find
the story has excitement (good plot) and a comfortable ending (things coming out all right).

One of the failures of research anent children and
their listening habits is in probing into the value of listening
to stories. Such a study is reported, however, in a recent
doctoral dissertation by Elsie Ziegler. [18] It reveals that chil-

dren exposed to activities in a creative dramatics program
did not show growth in reading interest or ability. Children
listening to stories, however, demonstrated significant gains
in these two areas. Children's librarians knew this all along!

Access to many resources is needed, and one must
turn to selection aids, not only to determine merit, but to
locate works--either the tales themselves or information about
material. New versions of folk tales are to be found in lists
of books by contemporary authors and artist-authors in The
Horn Book Magazine, which is one of the most reliable sources
for news of gems such as Verna Aardema's Why Mosquitos
Buzz in People's Ears and Beatrice Schenk De Regniers' Little Sister and the Month Brothers. Similar titles are found
here, reviewed by experienced critics. The Horn Book[19] is
the one publication that reviews current titles quickly and
well. Bibliographies found in texts, anthologies, and articles
on children's literature and storytelling come too late for the
impatient student who wants to know now.

Students ask a good question when they inquire why
writers on these subjects are slow to include the newer titles.
Errors in editing, also, may slow the student, leading the
searcher in the wrong direction.

In an attempt to arrange stories by levels, one collection states that "The Story of the Three Bears" and The
Jungle Book may be used with the same group. They may
go well together in the zoo, but it will be wise to keep them
separated in the story hour. This is certainly true when the
listeners are inexperienced.

After a story has been selected for telling, it is well
for the beginner to read several versions of the same story
if these exist. It is a rewarding exercise. For example:
although the variations in the actual body of "The Princess
on the Pea" are few, there are three different titles: the
one above, "The Real Princess," and "The Princess and the
Pea." Such irresponsible titling practices are confusing to
the beginner. Marie L. Shedlock, Valdemar Poulsen, Mrs.
Edgar V. Lucas, Erik Christian Haugaard, and Paul Leyssac
are among the translators who have had texts that included
this story.

Another type of variance is encountered in Harris'
"The Wonderful Tar-Baby." One editor, as noted above,
missed out completely when she did not know that the story

has two parts in the authoritative text, Uncle Remus: His
Songs and His Sayings. [20]   May Arbuthnot tried to rescue the
tar-baby by rewriting the story to omit the dialect, in Time
for Fairy Tales, Old and New. [21]   Gruenberg, also, has re-
fined the language, but (as others) has inadvertently left off
the last half of the story. [22]   The new versions lose something in this effort, however gracious it may be.

A beginner should study and compare such a situation
as three separate stories having a similar plot.   One case
involves the three stories, "Tom Tit Tot," "Rumpelstiltskin,"
and "Duffy and the Devil."   The first and third tales are
English variants, the first coming from Suffolk and the third,
from Devonshire, and labeled Cornish.   "Rumpelstiltskin,"
of course, is straight from the Grimm brothers although they
saw fit to spell it differently.

Jacobs does not hesitate to say that he prefers "Tom
Tit Tot" over "Rumpelstiltskin,"[23] but not all anthologists
are so inclined.   There are more good versions of the German story listed in catalogs than of the British variant, although Arbuthnot includes both of them in Time for Old Magic. [24]

This type of study is not necessary to telling either
version well, but some exploration of this nature should be
suggested to the apprentice in order to give body to the understanding of the art of selection.   As for "Duffy and the
Devil," no storyteller should be denied the privilege of knowing and appropriating with great glee, the Harve Zemach
presentation.

A lecturer can guide students as they study the art of
selection, and it is helpful to ask apprentices to state the
titles of their favorites and to discuss them.   The reminis-
cences of a variety of adults serve as stimulants to the whole
class, and the instructor can discover just how far along in
the story experience the students are.   The teacher should
show no sign of shock at learning how benighted some of today's students are, but one should attempt to help the beginner
overcome the lack of a personal storytelling heritage.

The instructor should pay close attention to the stories that are named since they represent the students' backgrounds: the stories they have read and heard, and the story
programs they may have given through formal telling, multimedia presentations, or reading aloud.

When storytellers are creative they can fashion a story
from a single chapter of a full-length book (if it can stand
being lifted from the whole). Even though the apprentice may
choose to limit him or herself to folktales for the first ex-
pedition into storytelling, here, too, one must exercise cau-
tion and do a little comparison-shopping among the multitude
of offerings.

Older boys and girls, and young adults, still searching for heroes, listen with an almost holy intensity to a well-
told story of a famous person who is a favorite of both the
teller and the listeners. It is challenging to combine parts
of two or more separate biographies when the various pass-
ages are found to complement each other; this activity borders
on the telling of original material which the storyteller may
have written.

Practice of this nature comes in handy when a full-
length book must be shortened without breaks in the story
line. One must be wary of striking sections that advance the
plot and give reasons for certain actions. Although most
folktales need no cutting, longer stories, novellas, and complete books must be treated to the shears. It is not difficult
to create phrases with the same words used by the author
and to piece out the gaps. When this is not possible, similar words and an imitative style can be employed if the sequence and the spirit of the tale are not lost.

The experienced storyteller may wish often to tell
personally created material, and at one time the National
Story League required its members to write and tell their
own stories at least once a year.

Sometimes it is necessary to create material from
primary sources to make special people or events come alive.
This takes a great deal of time and energy, and teachers and
librarians may find creative writing hard to reconcile with
their busy days and nights. Some who also write, find it
hard to tell their own stories. Since there are many examples of master storytellers doing just that, it could be
either that the hard-to-tell stories are not written well enough,
or that the storyteller is not skilled or objective enough in
presenting them.

The storyteller who enjoys writing and telling original
stories, however, will be able to polish and to add special
effects, and to fashion characterizations that will move the

action and refine the story content. This is a real opportunity for the teller to gain experience in letting a story flow, to add bits and pieces as they are coaxed out by the enthusiasm of the listeners.

During such an occasion a tape recorder (with the audience knowing it is on) can be used to get the story as it is told. A replay, with the gasps and the laughter, makes such an experience very personal and could excite even the most uninterested child. A second or third recording should show great improvement in the technique of the storyteller and point up efficacious pruning of the material. Too, the recording demonstrates--reassures the beginner about--the pleasure with which the story was received. A storyteller turned writer should be cautioned against allowing material to become too personalized unless the experiences are exceptional.

A storyteller has a unique opportunity when presenting a picture book with no words. Such an experience was shared by one children's librarian and a group of adults--and later, children: the story was one created by the storyteller who was motivated by the illustrated, non-verbal book, The Good Bird. [25] The adults found it difficult to relate to what was happening; the children knew exactly. They thought the stories they built and told aloud (after they had listened to the story by the speaker) were much superior!

Of such variety in action, the storyteller forms a background and begins a repertoire. A file with pertinent information such as sources, copies of edited material, the names of copyright owners, and publishers' addresses, and tapes and/or cassettes to show the stages of the teller's progress in writing and telling original material, and notes of evaluations of programs--all should be kept safe for instant use.

This private source of information points up again the "two strings to one's bow," and reduces the trauma of story selection. With one's own native good sense, a feel for appropriate material, with knowledge of what will be enjoyed, one may search out volumes by the dozens.

With the previewing being done by professionals, collections will be as failsafe as possible, and the storyteller may wander among the stacks finding much to like and to share. Let it be special. When it is shaped and molded, and spoken afresh by a storyteller who paints deftly in choice words, (both one's own and the author's), a living, strong message will come out.

NOTES

1. Jacobs: pp. 130-135.

2. Kipling, Just So... : pp. 63-84.

3. Finger: pp. 143-155.

4. Pyle: pp. 135-147.

5. Hutchinson: pp. 125-133.

6. Geisel (Dr. Seuss).

7. Ireland.

8. Hogrogian.

9. Kipling, Just So....

10. Sandburg: pp. 3-17.

11. Evidently no longer published as an individual volume; see Association for Childhood Education International: Told Under the Magic Umbrella, Edith Rickert, "The Bojabi Tree," pp. 101-112.

12. Bishop and Wiese.

13. Jacobs.

14. Schwartz: pp. 3-7.

15. Downs: pp. 181-185.

16. De Manpassant: pp. 61-68, pp. 137-144.

17. Ross: pp. 137-151.

18. Elsie Ziegler, "A Study of the Effects of Creative Dramatics...," Dissertation Abstracts International, 31: 648Z-A, June, 1971.

19.   Published by the Horn Book, Inc. , 585 Boylston Street, Boston, Mass. , 02116.

20.   Harris.

21.   Arbuthnot, <u>Time for Fairy Tales</u>...: pp. 216-218.

22.   Gruenberg: pp. 336-338.

23.   Jacobs: p. 244.

24.   Arbuthnot, <u>Time for Old Magic</u>: "Tom Tit Tot," pp. 19-21; "Rumpelstiltskin," pp. 72-74.

25.   Wezel.

Chapter Five

FASHIONING A HAPPENING

From the moment of decision, when the story to be
told has been selected, the storyteller begins to create a new
work of art. The first reading, during the period of selection, has alerted the teller to the appropriateness of the material for the specific occasion; its length, the style, and the
mood in which it is written; the plot, dominant characters,
and special phrases; and any special problems to be solved.
Additional early readings point up the significant action that
moves the plot along, the humor that lightens serious events,
and the sequences that appeal most to the teller.

The need for any editing or adapting soon emerges,
as well as whether or not there is any memorization necessary: rhymes, songs, lists of names of persons, places or
things, chants, quotations, or long, recurring descriptive
phrases found in cumulative tales.

Study of the material may be compared with an analysis of a happening, and one may call to mind the parts of
a news story. A conversation with a friend telling of an
event that has occurred in the home or neighborhood, or a
letter to a relative giving an account of an occasion such as
a party or a wedding, are similar in structure to most tales
one will select to learn over the years. The conversational
style in the telling is like that used to relate newsy events
to friends. One sees the comparison, understands the age-
old connection between newsgatherers and storytellers. As
one reads one identifies the sequences that make up the beginning, middle, and end of the story, and the storyteller
may wish to put on paper a diagram of the material that will
help in learning the selection.

The Funny Thing[1] is a light, humorous, yet precise,
tale of "Bobo, the good little man of the mountains," who
"at the door of his mountain cave" fed the squirrels, birds,

41

long-eared rabbits, and the little mice. Within its thousand
or so words it introduces two special surprises for its listeners: an animal who wants to be called an aminal and a
new word, "jum-jills," for the special food Bobo prepares
for it.   The surprise word is reminiscent of those created
by Edward Lear, Herman Melville, and Edith Rickert.

Bobo and the funny thing are the speaking characters;
the minor ones are the birds who, in the ending, feed jum-
jills to the aminal. The aminal has chosen to give up eating
good children's dolls and is content to sit, hardly moving, on
the top of the big mountain--necessary because its tail keeps
getting longer and longer. So, it sits, displaying the pretty
black eyebrows, the row of blue points down its back, and
the tail that grows and curls contentedly around the mountain.

After several readings, one identifies the first setting
to be in the mountains with the sun playing hide-and-seek;
fluffy floating clouds, soft warm air. A bit of extra charm,
relative to the beauty and the grandeur of the mountains, may
be added verbally when the listeners are living in coastal
areas. No introduction, of course, is necessary when the
audience is of the foothills or higher elevations, but recognition by the speaker of the closeness with the mountains,
implicit in the listeners, will kindle an even greater pride
in this experience than is already theirs. It helps, too, to
build a greater rapport between the storyteller and the audience.

The second setting is Bobo's home in a cave, and the
listener is delighted with the description of the floor plan of
the kitchen where Bobo makes up the various foods he prepares for the animals. The third set is the mountain top
that the aminal has chosen as the convenient place to house
itself and its tail as it eats more and more jum-jills.

To describe the little round balls that are "very good,"
the storyteller must remember the ingredients:

Jum-jills

7 nut cakes	2 cabbage salads
5 seed puddings	15 little cheeses

Mix with a spoon and roll into little round balls.
Place on a plate and feed to aminal.

The entire story can be easily followed in one's mind, for it unwinds the mountains, the sun, the clouds as gracefully as the unrolling of a film. Bobo is in front of the cave, waiting for the birds and the small animals who come for food. The names of the foods fed to each are easy to remember since both Bobo, and the listener, know the animals' preferences.

Into this idyllic scene comes the funny thing: something like a dog, a little like a giraffe. The special physical features of the aminal add to its uniqueness; its appetite for dolls is startling. Since Bobo cannot accept the aminal's taste for "good children's good dolls," he has to come up with a solution to this dilemma. After selling the funny thing the idea of the gourmet delight that will enhance the beauty of its eyebrows and tail, he mixes up a batch of jum-jills. All ends happily.

As one reads the picture story it is obvious that the illustrations carry many subtle drawings that are not incorporated into the tale: the furniture in the bedroom, the desk in the den, and the table and bowl in the kitchen. Since the storyteller desires to make the story vivid, satisfying, and cozy--like a doll's house--a simple mention of these familiar articles may be added to flesh out the text. One storyteller enjoys adding color to the bowl and giving a wooden texture to the spoon. With these, and a few other touches, she makes the telling her own particular creation without cheapening the folktale quality of the original theme.

While this particular story really needs nothing deleted nor added, some of these suggestions may be considered for their applicability to other stories. One notes that few gestures are indicated in The Funny Thing, but the storyteller may find the stirring together of the four ingredients irresistable. A firm line, however, must be drawn between these hand movements and any representation of the fluttering birds or the fluffy clouds.

The use of gestures can demonstrate the skill of the storyteller, but there is much negative regard of this practice. Experienced storytellers, however, with whom gestures are natural and who understand their tasteful use, discover more need for them in telling stories to the mentally handicapped. A good rule of thumb concerning gestures is that they can be used with additional pleasure for the listener when underscoring a sturdy, emphatic action. All delicate, fairy-like movement, or ethereal qualities of the story, should be left to the imagination. A hint of a gesture, a slight motion, is generally more effective and much more elegant.

The Funny Thing is a winner for beginners and experienced storytellers, and is well-received by listeners from any ethnic background. Most children have made friends with imaginary animals, and listeners are always caught up in the outsmarting of a villain however much like a pussy cat the miscreant may become. The use of flattery is practiced by everyone at some time.

This story, as many other original themes and folktales, may be dressed up or down. The ending can be faded back into the same sunshiny day the story opened with. Real magic has been sensed. It was really once-there-was-and-was-not; who is to say really which?

This feeling out of the salient points--or imaginative possibilities--of a story may be repeated in getting acquainted with any new material. Attention paid to identifying special features or nuances maximizes the strength of a good story and does not interfere with the smooth learning of it.

Presently, many storytellers are selecting pictured tales in a similar format and find Marcia Brown, Janina Domanska, Paul Galdone, Nonny Hogrogian, Ezra Jack Keats, Blair Lent, Leo Lionni, Evaline Ness, and Maurice Sendak marvelous partners in the fun.

After several readings, if major editing is indicated, it is important to reassess the story for possible replacement by a simplified version, if one can be found. One may decide to search for an entirely different tale. However, when one feels capable of improvisation this may be attempted. The storyteller must be careful to preserve the style, purpose, and mood, as well as the freshness that the author has created in the original material. A study of all sequences must follow so that no clue, no important detail is omitted.

It is advisable for the apprentice to think carefully before attempting revision, but the novice must begin sometime to practice this skill. Material that presents more problems than pleasure, however, should be rejected. There are too many wonderful tales begging to be told for any storyteller to have to worry about shortening, adapting, changing, or forcing material to fit a given pattern or occasion.

In the 1930's when storytelling was, perhaps, at its
height, teachers and librarians were trained to tell stories
by being advised to just read and read; to reread and reread;
and to tell the story aloud to oneself (or to anyone who might
be willing to listen) over and over again. But once it is understood that catching the flavor of a tale is the most important step, it is easy enough to read up on newer suggestions,
and then to devise one's own method.

The recreative method, discussed and approved over
a half-century ago by the authors of A Handbook of Children's
Literature,[2] was basic to the techniques used by many library-
trained storytellers of that period.   Some parts of the story
were remembered, some memorized.   It may be well to experiment with several methods to ascertain which works best
for the individual learner.   One must always keep in mind
never to be afraid of a story.   Jotting down an analysis of
the tale, with a diagram, or placing sequences in word-panels
is an easy way to begin.

Most experts advise against memorization of the material word by word, although some storytellers come to this
approach naturally.   The warning comes in all sincerity since
the inexperienced may surely stumble over lines at one time
or another.

Too much emphasis against "dramatics" in a story
presentation may have been given also. The storyteller should
remember that the story must sparkle to impress the listener.
To learn how to tell a tale with flair is a step in the right
direction.   When the storyteller has a gift for the dramatic,
and this gift is trained and controlled, the presentations,
like the little bear's porridge, should be just right.

Critics tend to confuse dramatization with artificial
enthusiasm and a vague disrespect of the material. . Nevertheless, it is during the preparation of a story that these decisions must be made.   A storyteller does not have to ago-
nize over these problems when learning each new story.
Once a satisfactory method is developed the business of mastering material will come naturally and automatically, and
one will get on with the show.

Now that classes in storytelling are prevalent; when
the learning process is made more understandable and easier, it is a shame that fewer teachers and librarians working with children care to become storytellers.

If fear of learning stories to tell is responsible for
the paucity in numbers of storytellers, here are some suggestions to slay the dragon.   The study procedure should begin with pleasure and anticipation, and one should become
familiar with the material through analysis of its parts and
visualization of the sequences in logical order.   Any needed
changes in text should be made, and a copy of the story as
it will be learned should be typed, taped, or prepared in
some more or less permanent form.   Purchase of the original material will allow changes to be made directly onto
the page, and this ensures its availability for future programs.

A tape of the story is of value in several ways: one
is able to listen to oneself, to be one's own audience; to listen for conversational, natural dialogue; to judge the use of
pauses, the overall pace of the story, and one's breathing
habits.   Breathing and swallowing faults are common--and
noticeable--and any habit that detracts from a presentation
must be of concern to the storyteller.   Listening to a tape
is also good for anchoring the story as a whole.   Awkward
hesitations caused by searching for the correct word can be
noted, and eliminated through a quick look at the text and
more practice.   A videotape of a work period is invaluable,
and an opportunity to make one should be made available to
each student in a formal study program.

Some storytellers carry the material around with them,
snatching peeks at a free moment, but one must be careful
not to misplace the book!   Some have been so engrossed in
mumbling a story--while driving--that the police have added
their own sequence to the tale.   Such attempts to get close
to a story may be tempting, but they are not to be condoned.
Several periods of total concentration will serve, preventing
possible upsets on the freeway.

One hears much about mental pictures being allowed
to run through the mind, but of equal importance is the "hearing" of dialogue.   What one sees and hears is what is shared.
This step will fix the words belonging to the action, also
pointing up what gestures the characters might use in speaking in the imagined scene.   Too, any necessary voice changes
may become obvious.   One should not, however, begin too
early to fit words to action.   This synthesis may come naturally; give it a chance.   Before one goes to sleep at night
and upon awakening in the morning are excellent times to
run through the material.

The apprentice should not hesitate to break up a story
to learn it. Beginning to live with certain bits of action and
dialogue and then adding more provides the sort of closeness
that enables the student to feel completely at home with the
tale. Good concentration while reading, both silently and a-
loud, will cement certain descriptive words or phrases forever to delineate specific characters, settings, and action;
in this way the part-by-part approach will not confuse.

Logical transitional phrases will connect sections of
the plot when one sees the story as a whole. Add light touches
to make the presentation one's own. Consider the effective
gestures, pay attention to the pause, do pantomime, especially
in folktale material, and do not forego--nor disparage--the
dash of dramatic flair.

When there are several important characters, one of
the lesser figures may be chosen to help set atmosphere,
mood, and pace. In learning "Molly Whuppie" one storyteller
selects the giant's wife as guide to help set the mood of the
night's drawing in, the darkness of the forest, and the mystery of the house in the wood. At the conclusion of the story,
the giant's wife is prominent in a humorous sequence that
lightens an otherwise fierce ending. This tale is an excellent one to choose to study the various methods of learning
material. One could never be bored with Molly.

Some storytellers find it helpful to practice in front
of a mirror; if a storyteller can face that (even with some
merriment), she or he should be able to face anyone! This
procedure is also helpful to an inexperienced student in learning to tolerate more quickly minor disturbances that may a-
rise during a presentation. Such experience is necessary
when preparing material for television and a practice session
on videotape is not possible. The storyteller will have some
definite picture of what the viewers are seeing and will not
keep searching for the monitor.

The mirror lets the storyteller know which gestures
are natural, which are not, and those that should be retained
to serve as catalysts (taking nothing away but clarifying and
speeding action). Clever, significant gestures may be compared with the signature of an artist on a painting, the selahs
of the Bible, and the rhymed couplets Shakespeare used to
herald the conclusion of many scenes and acts.

A story may actually come alive through one particu-

larly clever gesture or the repetition of a motion used in
telling a cumulative tale.   This is true of the tactile relationship between the blind men and the elephant; the "tsk,
tsk, tsk," of the peddler and the monkeys' imitations.

Storytelling calls for all the skills of a good speaker,
and the greater one's gifts of selection and presentation, the
more seriously one should approach the fashioning of a story.
It is at the learning step that the storyteller is most often
spooked and stumbles.   A check of the literature shows no
written method guaranteeing an instant flawless story so that
a listener may live happily ever after.   The storyteller still
has to devise a workable way to furnish the desired results.

However, emphasis on the learning process should be
treated in depth to assure the apprentice that every storyteller is afraid of failure at some time in the story experience.   This fear evolves from the notion that one may not
be able to compete with the visual entertainment and the
fast-paced lifestyle of even the very young.

Apprentice storytellers are also unsure of their being
able to hold an audience of any kind.   The novice may be
excused for this fear: it is only human to want success.
Any distrust of oneself in the storytelling process should be
used as an incentive to prepare the material properly, to
spend more time in selection, to approach the learning experience with more pleasure, and in a happier, more relaxed
state of mind.

The viewing of two films will help the apprentice to
become acquainted with techniques used by accomplished
storytellers: "There's Something About a Story" and "The
Art of Telling Stories to Children."[3]   These films are often
shown to classes in storytelling, and students say they encourage and give support in the mastering of the art.

The films also demonstrate that anyone who is truly
interested need not feel dread nor fear drudgery.   The films
portray many examples of adults enjoying the story experience:
selecting the story, planning the presentation, shaping the
material, and letting it all burst forth in joy.

NOTES

1.   Gág.

2.   Gardener and Ramsey: pp. 40-44.

3.   See under their titles in the FILM part of the Bibliography.

Chapter Six

"ONCE UPON A TIME..."

No one discounts the desirability of attractive packaging of merchandise, and meticulous care is taken with items to be presented as gifts. So must the gift of a story be wrapped in a tissue of mystery and tied with a magic bow. The enchantment begins with the setting of a mood, relaxed but expectant. Every visible person and object, each audible sound has its own particular role. Precautions to assure a convenient, comfortable time and place, and an enthusiastic person for the telling, have been taken. The wheels of every scrap of machinery have been oiled and inspected. The moment is now, and all evidence of work, planning, and preparation has disappeared.

The storyteller, tastefully and unobtrusively dressed, has arrived early and is eager to greet the guests with warmth. There should be no final flurry of activity, no loud acclaims of a forgotten duty, nor last exchanges of talk with another adult. The story hour has begun.

As the audience gathers, the storyteller is sorting out who will enjoy the story most, and who the least; who will savor every word, who will become bored and restless. The storyteller (if a guest) will have arranged for a short, or better, no introduction, unless the audience is primarily adult. When the storyteller is no stranger to the group, one is in clover.

This is the perfect time for the story to begin. The story hour symbols are in place (if they are to be used): the candle is burning, the music is silenced; coats and purses are stowed under the chairs or are on the floor beside the listeners and their cushions. The fresh flowers are a bright spot; the display books, if any, are arranged conveniently near. How elegant if it is winter and there is the added luxury of a blazing, saffron fire on a big stone hearth.

50

If favors or food, treats of any kind, are to be a
part of the affair, they should not be on display in sight of
the group, especially, if the audience is predominantly children. Goodies are distracting, so any announcements of a
party to follow are made after the stories.

During a holiday season, a storyteller was pressured
into telling "one more story" to aid a group of adults who
were a bit slow in preparing refreshments in a room separate from the program. As soon as the helpers had finished
their preparations, a door behind the storyteller (who, of
course, was right at a most exciting place) was flung open
and a loud and happy invitation was called for the children
to "Come and get it!" The poor storyteller was almost
crushed by the enthusiastic audience rushing for the eats.
This situation could have been minimized if the storyteller
had thought to stand facing the door.

The pause, between the last necessary noise of the
settling down and the first noises that denote a restlessness
for the program to begin, is similar to the instant the quarter-
back calls for the football to be snapped into play: this is
the moment that counts. Introductions or information about
the story must be given to the audience as part of the story
itself and should include only what is absolutely necessary.
Explanation of unfamiliar words can be accomplished easily
by giving immediately after uttering the word, a short throwaway definition.

Librarians once belabored a storyteller who was demonstrating storytelling to them for not explaining the word
"yam" used by Courlander in his story "Talk." Being from
the Southern part of the world, the storyteller had never considered this word unfamiliar, but the incident could have been
avoided by her adding, after "yam," the first time around,
which in the text appears in the plural, "sweet potatoes!"
The handling of problems such as this, and of any surly or
disruptive attitudes, have been perfectly dealt with in "The
Story-Teller" by Saki--a story all storytellers should discover
for their amusement and profit.

When the storyteller has planned to seek special support from the audience with a straightforward request, this
may be accomplished early on, but hard on its heels comes
the opening of the story, spoken softly, distinctly, and with
enthusiasm. The speaker begins with a hint of magic and
joy, "Once there was," "Once upon a time," "There was

once," "Long, long ago," or a borrowed beginning from Kipling or Wilde, but never with an opening that asks a question. The storyteller may develop a special beginning that can be used many times during a long career: the introduction of invisible friends or a pantomime of the opening of a bag of tricks or gifts.

One day, a storyteller who enjoyed starting with a pantomime of the flicking from her right forefinger, the invisible Tyll,[1] and from her left, the fairy Tillette,[2] was telling stories to children and teachers in the auditorium of a large elementary school. She sent the invisible friends to chat together near a flowerpot sitting in a window to her left, behind where she stood. All went well until an unnoticed vibration, somewhere in the old building, managed to dislodge the pot, sending it with a scraping sound from the ledge to the ground below. She says that from that day, when she would meet any of the kids or teachers from that school, they walked judiciously around her, asking if she had her invisible friends along.

A magical inference may be used to quiet lively young listeners, and a perfect passage to paraphrase is the bewitching "the sound ... was the sound of the grass growing or the corn ripening or the holly reddening--which is to say no sound at all."[3] This is the noise one may subtly suggest be made by the youngsters. (Ruth Sawyer never fails the storyteller.) Now, the speaker catches the eyes of the audience and looks deeply into each pair. Also during a story, a friendly, understanding glance into the right set of eyes will silence an eager tongue or still a wandering hand (or foot) seeking expression.

The eyes have it--and sometimes unexpectedly so. Once a storyteller visited a branch library in a Finnish neighborhood of a large city. She had come through a deep fall of snow, but she was ready. Part way through the first story she felt an unsettling sensation. Something was wrong. The experience was different from any she had ever had. She looked again at the children. Silently, she questioned each pair of bright eyes looking into hers. Without breaking the rhythm of the story, she became more and more disquieted. All at once she laughed out loud. Each pair of eyes in front of her--were blue! Bright blue, crystal-sparkling eyes: the mystery was solved.

Yes, the eyes have it, but so do the hands. It is

said that a greater proportion of the brain is devoted to the
control of the hands than to any other part of the body. The
hands are clever, expressive, suggestive, quick, furtive, and
even the merest motion from one can create a mood. A hand,
even one finger, can summon, reject, accuse, command, emphasize, point up, point down, and admonish.

  The use of the head may also highlight portions of a
story. Too much use of the body, however, may distract or
beguile the audience. When gesturing comes easily, it can
strengthen characterization. A child-audience, especially one
composed of kids living in the central city, needs gestures.
These children, sadly enough, are more accustomed to pushes,
punches, and distorted faces than they are to a verbal request
or courteous directions. Rule One, however, in gesturing is
that the gesture always precedes the word or phrase it em-
phasizes.

  Much is written anent the use of the voice, the training of it, and how one's breathing patterns may be improved
to enhance delivery. Pitch, enunciation, and breath control
are three of the areas for study. Storytellers who have no
obvious accent nor sectional drawl--no impediment--are fortunate, but listening to a tape of one's voice will quickly identify any problems to be resolved. Ruth Sawyer, Ruth Tooze,
and Caroline Bauer have all[4] written well on this subject, and
the apprentice should seek out and study their exercises and
suggestions for conquering any bad habits.

  Reading aloud to oneself, to a friend, speaking into a
tape recorder, making discs for radio programs and hearing
these played back, all are good ways to know how one's voice
sounds to others. The storyteller may practice certain vowels
and word-endings as a singer would run scales. Of first importance is that the storytellers speak distinctly and project
their voices so that each person in the audience may be able
to hear the softest whisper.

  Acoustics in many school and library conference and
meeting rooms leave much to be desired. Lack of funds for
improvement is a problem for storyteller and audience alike;
the storyteller who can act in a leadership role should work
toward improvement in the story-hour environment. In the
meantime, the storyteller is responsible for being heard in
every corner of the area regardless of the size of the room
or number of listeners in the audience.

Manipulation of the voice to aid character impersonation should be used sparingly, but apprentices will want to sharpen their skills in this direction whether or not they choose to employ this technique. Substitutions, for impersonations, are abbreviated gestures that hint of a certain trait, and phrases that can identify various characters. Voice changes are effective, and they need not be sustained throughout the entire story. Any distinctive voice trick or mimicry should be maintained consistently and forcefully, however, for the moments it is in use.

During a radio presentation when gestures can help only to put the storyteller in a mood, the voice does take on added significance since through this medium, the actual gestures mean nothing to the invisible audience.

Gesturing has largely gone wrong, probably because elocutionists in the early twentieth century (recitation and declamation contests compounding the crime) over-used this technique. Voice changes and gestures when natural, however, can demonstrate the skills of storytelling, and set the better practitioners apart from those with less bent toward the art. Moderation in their use is still the key to good taste and welcome reception. Instructors are quick to spot the student who has that something extra and should be allowed and encouraged to use it.

Body language, sometimes unconsciously expressed by the storyteller, is well understood by the listeners, and is a major influence in the impression being made. In these silent mannerisms the audience is quick to see, and to measure, their purpose and effect, and can judge to what extent the speaker is sincerely and intimately involved in the experience. The use of the body exhibits innate reactions, and it communicates a sophisticated honoring of silence. Through it, the storyteller allows glimpses of the characters in their relationships with each other as they perform actions that advance the plot.

In "Molly Whuppie," the giant's "business" of assembling the scissors, needle and thread, thimble, and other items, strengthens the interaction between Molly and the giant and gives mental images with which the listeners may work as they reconstruct the scene for themselves. This interplay between the giant and Molly is similar to that occurring between the storyteller and the group. The audience is now at one with the speaker, but it also functions as so many sep-

arate individuals, each producing a special, private "showing."
The approach using minimal pantomime and invisible stage
properties, can give a tremendous boost to simplifying the
story-learning process as well as incurring the pleasure of
the later listeners.

Pantomime, while it accomplishes stage business, also
aids in the pacing of a story. Since pace is influenced by
plot development and the movement of characters, as well as
the writer's use of action verbs and the natural rate of speech
of the storyteller, one can see the obvious correlation of pacing and the stage admonition of picking up one's cues. The
extent to which one is able to interpret the "business" of the
characters is just so far as the storyteller is able to flesh
out a solid experience for an audience, and it is only during
such procedures, which reinforce the pantomime with realism,
that the speaker's eyes ever leave the listeners.

With the audience as an important motivating force, an
effective pace may be achieved. One hot Texas afternoon, a
storyteller was recreating the myth of Jason and the Golden
Fleece. She was weary with the heat and the arduous adventures of Jason, herself, but suddenly she caught sight of a
small Mexican American who though following Jason avidly
all the way, nevertheless looked distinctly uncomfortable. As
Jason accomplished one exploit after another, the small face
and hands became more and more expressive. The child was
almost standing, was shaking with expectancy. The storyteller sensed an urgency to wrap up the story but then she
saw his hands seek the lower front of his body, kneading his
groin. The storyteller increased her pace, and, finally, as
she tells it now, spoke the ending: "Jason grabbed the golden
fleece, jumped on board the Argo, and sailed away."

She saw the young lad grab himself, dance up and down,
and run from the room, shouting, "Jesus Christ! He made
it! He made it!" Acceleration of pace had saved the day.
Regardless of children and their physical needs, a storyteller
should increase slightly the tempo as the tale winds down.

Before experiencing the delicious sensation of having
successfully concluded a story, apprentices may have a
healthy (and valid) fear of their ability to hold an audience
of children. Students ask over and over what artifices may
be used to minimize disruptions by the restless, but observant
storytellers, arriving early, would have already spotted the
possible troublemakers.

A short, arresting story, with a new twist, may be told before the main story in order to test the mood of the assembly. "Teeny Tiny" and "Master of All Masters" are good ones to use. A bit of poetry may be said if it is brief and carries a taste of humor. The something special that will insure the cooperation of the listeners is the warmth and the aura of caring cast by the storyteller, and the general sense of festival.

It should not be necessary during a story to have to fall back on the questionable technique of calling the miscreants' names to get their attention. The squeaking wheel should not always get the oil. It is a poor show to ruin the story experience for others in the attempt to soothe one or a few savage breasts by breaking the spell and talking to them. Catching the eye of the potential problem child may be all that is needed. A sly wink denotes a closeness and a sharing of something intimate between the one child and the speaker. It is friendly and in no way should it convey a correction or a reprimand. The result is that the one seeking special attention receives it from the adult, and the child may read into this private exchange any desired solace. The secret of resolution, however, lies in the ability of storytellers to handle themselves during a disturbance of any nature.

In a small group one may be able quickly to identify potential disrupters, and to reach out to embrace or to move closer to them. One morning about twenty-five three- and four-year-olds were being shown a new large mediamobile. Nothing satisfied them, however, until they were promised a story. On the carpeted floor the children gathered happily, but there was one bouncy, friendly youngster to whom all of this was so new, so thrilling, that he could not contain his exuberance. Jumping up and down, to judge whether or not he could dislodge the books from the walls of the vehicle, was more exciting to the lad than just sitting and listening to any story. The storyteller reached for him, pulled him down gently, and, enveloping him in the crook of her left arm, she continued with the story just begun. This action is an age-old device, and it has great merit.

One should give serious thought to whether or not one will sit or stand to tell stories. The seated storyteller in the incident noted above was definitely at an advantage as she held the child; while standing, however, at the first of the story, she was able to initiate quick action. One does learn to adapt!

The position in which one tells a story is not always left to the preference of a storyteller. Large groups need to see, and standing is correct at such a time. Sitting with a small group may be acceptable, but one loses many opportunities for body language. One storyteller has confided that standing is safer. She tells a story that when she was working with some small children once, and sitting with a child with wet pants on her left knee, a second child crawled near and whispered as he poked her right knee, "You've got two laps!" He promptly sat down and took advantage of this discovery.

So, the most disastrous result of poor handling of discipline problems is when the storyteller blows both cool and cover. Instead, one should use the voice: lowering, not raising it; attempt even stronger but quieter enthusiasm, and as far as possible, accept events as they develop. Overt actions, not associated with the story, and spoken corrections, out of character, are dangerous ploys for the apprentice. The experienced storyteller seldom has to resort to them.

For reassurance for the speaker, some old hands suggest that a storyteller select (in her or his own mind) one member of the group and let that person represent the listeners. A particular individual's reactions may indicate the mien and responsiveness of the audience. Ignoring the not-too-naughty has also been found to discourage disruptions.

The most disruptive influence on children being told stories are the adults who accompany them. They often do not care to sit and be a part of the scene, but since their sense of responsibility is strong, they remain. Then there is often much talking, getting up and down, reminding, and waving of hands and fingers in attempts to correct behavior. These verbal and physical interjections are more annoying than the whispers that demonstrate a release of tension building from the expected excitement to come.

Adults are afraid that the kids will not reflect the good manners they have been taught, so they are anxious during the "performance." But the solution is not for the adults to be excluded from the audience. One has only to say courteously before the stories begin that the storyteller will be glad to handle all discipline, is in charge of the situation, and that the grown-ups are to relax and enjoy the program as listeners. Story hours go well more often than they do not.

Stock endings are attached to most folktales: "They lived happily ever after," "If they didn't live happily ever after, it is nothing to you nor me," "And that's all" are beloved ones. Most writers of original themes add a throwaway line to their stories, too, but the storyteller may choose to add a favorite ending borrowed from a particular writer or tale--one that has become a sort of verbal signature. The ending has special significance since it serves to lift down the listeners to normal ground level, easing the flight from the stars, placing them firmly back on earth.

Although it may seem a bit immodest for the storyteller to prepare an audience to applaud, when the assembly is composed mainly of children, it is wise to have the listeners participate in a general move to show appreciation of the story. Girls and boys should be taught that they are partners through to the end of the presentation, and that the speaker is due a vote of confidence. This procedure is recommended not solely for the purpose of showing thanks to the storyteller alone, but to begin to shape young followers to appreciate any public speaker or entertainer. Children who are regulars at story hour are learning to function as a group, and they make good listeners for singers, instrumentalists, and others.

When performers are not applauded today, it is not always that they have not amused nor entertained well, but that audiences do not know that this show of pleasure is appropriate.

Clapping for a good story is a much more mature ending to the affair than for the storyteller to begin to inquire if the listeners have had a good time. The storyteller should not expect instant reaction to the story, and should not indulge in the too-common practice of expecting a child audience to want to jump up and act out the stories or to grab a crayon and begin to illustrate what they have experienced.

The storyteller should be good enough to have left some positive impression, but some listeners are slow to get it all straight, and may want to savor the stories a bit longer. It is quite rude to expect a verbal or motor reaction.

When the flurry of conversation and coughing has passed, the stretching completed, the applause subsided, the storyteller may invite the audience to browse if books are available. Unless the storyteller is quite familiar with the audience, it may be decided that books will not be recom-

mended at this time. Books so often spell failure to many
children; especially those of the inner-city.

The invitation to look at and to borrow books should
be just that--an invitation. Some listeners come for the
story; they aren't readers, and they may have to be wooed
patiently through means other than storytelling gatherings.
The story hour is one of the true entertainments, and it should
not be used as a gimmick. Here, the wheels of the machinery must be very quiet indeed. Ulterior motives to increase
readership, however altruistic, must not be obvious.

It certainly is not wise to introduce a table of books
before the story. Although the story hour leads toward books
and reading, of course, subtlety must be allowed to win the
day. Adult audiences are different: they do not see themselves as targets for an eager pedagogue. They do not feel
(or at least not so often) that they are being manipulated, as
children sometimes do. So, beware the book with some chil-
dren--one will know when the time comes.

Books pressed upon a group ready for a story may
set a wrong mood; books afterward, may be anticlimactical,
destroying a feeling or set of images left in the listeners'
imaginations. The story hour is to entertain; it is not a
come-on to force a child into a lifetime of serfdom, as some
have been heard to say, to the printed word. The storyteller
would be wiser to excuse the audience, with the blowing out
of the candle and the wishing, if such had been arranged, and
then to enter into a search for good books, to say goodbyes,
or to listen to the children who want personally to express
appreciation for the event or to ask a question or just to chat.

When children are first introduced to story hour, it is
well that the storyteller explain to them that it is courteous,
and much appreciated by the storyteller--or any other entertainer or host--for them to say a word of farewell as they
leave. Many children who are shy with words, or don't know
exactly what to say, may wish to touch the adult who has
pleased them. Many children hunger for closeness and will
automatically, with pleasure, hug the storyteller, sometimes
causing embarrassment and uncomfortableness. Regardless
of the reaction the children exhibit, the storyteller should allow the response to be individual and spontaneous, but over-
exuberance should be courteously (but quickly) terminated.

At the conclusion of the story hour, storytellers have

given their all; they are tired and all-passion spent, and, for some, there may be a second group waiting. If a second telling is expected, the apprentice would do well to have prepared a different program of material. Repeating the same stories is tiring--more tiring than changing about and introducing a new set of characters and plots. Even professional storytellers grow weary after a while, and they are not only better equipped but more accustomed to going on and on.

Storytelling is hard work, but the apprentice must not become discouraged, since the rewards are unbelievably sweet.

NOTES

1. Jagendorf.

2. Harper: Frank R. Stockton, "The Poor Count's Christmas," pp. 44-54.

3. Sawyer, Long Christmas: pp. 41-42.

4. Sawyer, The Way of...: pp. 88-89, pp. 131-138; Tooze: p. 17, pp. 41-44; Bauer: pp. 55-58.

Chapter Seven

"... LIVED HAPPILY EVER AFTER. "

The End! All the parts of storytelling are but a prelude to the moment the storyteller brings the story to its conclusion. The atmosphere is charged with feelings--and these
are what the listeners will take away. A brief pause, while
the storyteller stands quietly, smiling, is necessary to allow
the audience to come down to earth, reorienting itself into
the everyday world.

This speck of time is most poignant for storytellers.
They have sought to add a new dimension to the lives of the
listeners and they yearn to know the response. The final
words may have been those written, or the storyteller may
have added others. The ending may have been clever--one
that attached the original "signature" to the tale--or, it may
have directed the listener away from the last seconds of heavy
emotion. The conclusion may have set all to rights, or it
may have left the solution to the audience as Frank Stockton
did in "The Lady or the Tiger," or Saki in "The Open Window" and "Tobermory. "

The ending may be a surprise one such as Joseph
Jacobs uses in "Teeny Tiny. " The storyteller may make a
sudden gesture as Mark Twain wrote that he enjoyed doing. [1]
Many variations are acceptable, but each should give a fore-
taste of the future, a good example of which is the classic,
"... and they lived happily ever after. " The last sentence
may sum up what has gone before, or it may repeat what the
audience thinks--that the incident is over, and all is well.

Whatever the story's ending may have been, storytellers
want to know what the story has meant to the audience. This
mystery, however, is not often solved immediately and may
in fact be long in coming. Verbal response should not be requested openly. Storytellers must train themselves to be

courteous and allow individual persons to make any comment
they may wish to speak, or to keep silent. The storyteller
must remember that the true value of the experience cannot
be summed up quickly. One's own reaction to the material,
when it was first read and selected, will give some hint to
its reception. What reaction did one wish to set in motion?
The speaker may have wanted the audience to gain a feeling
of gaiety, or a deep sense of wonder. If it were a pleasant
feeling of being in on a secret, a new kinship with beauty, or
a bit of magic, probing into the minds of the audience would
add up to bad manners or worse. Facial expressions and
body language surely gave some indication, during the presentation, of delight or boredom. Wanting to know what the
listener will take away is natural and a worthy desire, but
what lingers with the listener, what accrues to the child or
adult, is of a personal nature.

It is the right of listeners to feel pain with the characters who suffer, to share indignation with them as well as
the glory of achievement and success. This is true participation.

In the sharing of these emotions, the listeners have
gone deep into their own lives. Some have felt compassion
for the first time, and are struggling to give this feeling a
name. Others may have partially left the story scene, looking into their own frustrations; to have entered the intimate
world of problem-solving. These reactions can only be shared
with a storyteller and a group through an honest "thank you"
or a mild exclamation of pleasure. Some of the audience,
however, may leave humming a bit of a song used in the
story, or repeating a snatch of rhyme, or a melodic or amusing phrase.

Through these actions the storyteller may know that
the listeners were awake, that something was heard and relished, and that an indescribable impression had been made.
But the storyteller should ask no questions. Responses will
be written on the faces of the group as it makes its way to
the exit, and at this moment, plainly described, is the evidence of the speaker's success or sentence.

One can hope that the listeners will reflect some inner
light that points up new-found knowledge, new solutions, or
pleasure. This richness in expression is far greater than a
coerced and badly executed sketch of Rapunzel as she lets
down her hair or a drawing of Little Red Riding Hood skipping

through the forest (with or without the wolf). Why do some storytellers request concrete evidence that children have shared stories with them?

Storytellers seldom ask adult audiences to react to a story program unless a request has been made, and time has been arranged, for an exchange of ideas stimulated by the material. When the story has been a selection from full-length books--for example A Separate Peace by John Knowles, John Steinbeck's The Red Pony and Travels with Charley, and Henry Roth's Call It Sleep--the audience may be eager to discuss the serious issues raised. Unless the plan has been to conclude the session with questions, answers, and a general discussion, the speaker should talk only with the small number who may care to remain after the program. If it is convenient, an informal period could be shared. The storyteller should neither expect nor demand comments.

Neither should the storyteller become involved with one or two members of the group to the exclusion of others who may have wanted the opportunity to talk. If any one wants to stay for further talk, he or she may be invited to do so at the discretion of the speaker. Listeners may wish to know the titles of some additional books similar to the ones from which the stories have been taken, and the speaker may provide a short list prepared in anticipation of such a request. However, a pleasant good night and a thank you are always proper.

For any type of audience, if the program has been held in a library or a bookstore, where books may be available, a selection of titles may be arranged for circulation or for purchase. The usual practice of having available copies of the titles used is not always sound. If there are few copies and the assembly is large, these should not be handed over to the first listener who may scramble to secure one for home reading. When possible, copies of the material may be put in an easily accessible place to aid the staff at a charge-out point. Arrangement to reserve copies in demand may be implemented if there are time and staff.

Since it is not good business ethics to advertise a product that cannot be supplied, a storyteller should not select a story program of material, if at least a part of it cannot be duplicated from among the holdings of the sponsoring agency.

Whatever the occasion, the purpose of the story program will control what, if anything, is to follow the stories. Although it must be kept constantly in mind that the purpose of storytelling is entertainment, sometimes the very nature of the material itself will call for additional activity.

When a story has been told only to acquaint the listeners with the plot, in order that creative dramatics may be enjoyed, the children are prepared to continue, moving with ease into another expression of the arts. The story presentation in this instance is not true storytelling, but an experience in creative dramatics with, of course, a story involved. The adviser should be sensitive to the wishes of the group, and one should adhere closely to the arranged plans since they are the guide that has been accepted by the participants, their parents, or whoever may be also concerned with arrangements. Also, an audience having just heard a story presentation in the regular pattern may also wish to act out the story. Here again, the adult in charge makes the decision.

At the conclusion of a story to a school group, in a classroom, the storyteller (guest, librarian, teacher) should not leave the students with a feeling that the story is part of a lesson. The recitation of poetry, when such activity falls within the context of a similar situation, has often been associated with a growing dislike of poetry for many. Listening to stories should be kept separate from any activity that may follow.

A period set aside for free expression, as an extension of a story and its creation in another art form could be enjoyable and worthwhile, but if in truth a free time is what is expected, it should remain just that. Any follow-up such as a reproduction of the plot in any form should be continued only if clamored for by the listeners. Even young children may want to talk about a story they have enjoyed.

Lucky is the teacher or librarian who meets often enough with the same children or adults to have learned preferences at such a moment. Experimentation with free periods is of inestimable value to all, and the results that come unsolicited are superbly satisfying.

In a public library situation what follows a story hour may be another story, a film, or a time for selection of material for reading at home. Whatever activity may be planned, to demand response is unforgivable.

An opportunity to visit with other participants in the
program may be offered, especially if a small snack is to be
given or a social hour is planned.   Adults enjoy chatting together, why not children?   Signing a guestbook may be fun,
too.   The period after the story may be profitably used by
issuing an invitation to browse in the library, to ask questions about borrowing, to seek answers to reference questions,
or to receive information on other services offered.   When
this type of activity is initiated, it is easy to understand why
it is necessary that the storyteller be familiar with the sponsoring agency and its facilities.   It is obvious that guest storytellers (or volunteers), unless they are trained, cannot function with assurance in answering library-related questions.
Attention may be called to a sign announcing the next story
hour; the group may be reminded of it as they finally leave
the story room.   No member of the group should be singled
out for special prodding to become a borrower or to participate in any specific activity.   Hearing the story may be the
only thing the listener came for.   A sincere invitation to return is enough for a first-timer.   Listeners will be quick to
ask for borrowers' cards when this is the purpose of the visit.

Sometimes a group of first-timers may become so
exuberant, or so intrigued with themselves, that when the
presentation is over, they will press for special attention.
One storyteller accepted such an episode as a challenge to
deal with an unspoken--but obvious--call for help.   She asked
the gang to remain after the others had gone and suggested
that since they were older than the regular audience, and
that they had different interests (diplomatic lady), perhaps
they would like their own program.   How would they like to
form a club?   She had guessed correctly; the kids agreed
with alacrity.

They returned, talked it over, organized a weekly,
evening storytime for young adults (they were all teen-age
males).   The young men chose a name, a regular time for
meeting, and the club lasted until the children's librarian was
transferred to another branch library.   These young men were
mostly foreign-born, living in the inner city.   They not only
listened to stories, but they wanted to sharpen their language
skills, become citizens, and at the same time to reminisce
about their native countries.

Another similar disruptive crowd decided when invited
to form a club and to write their own stories.   The storyteller welcomed them as young writers, and the library staff

encouraged their efforts as "reporters" of the news in the
community surrounding the library.   A trip to the largest
local newspaper was organized, and for a while these youngsters published their own mimeographed news sheet.   The
story hour in public libraries may be the source of new ideas
for activities for several age groups or for out-reach projects
that can make friends for the library, and may become core
groups for initiating special funding possibilities.   The story
hour is an important part of the public relations planning
since it offers a service to all age levels and can be developed to meet many interests.

It is difficult sometimes to fathom just what can come
from a storytime.   Frequently there are separate and very
personal reactions to storytelling long after the story experience.   One afternoon, standing on a curb at a busy intersection in a large Midwestern city, a storyteller was greeted by
a youngster who said, "Tell it again!"   Through some miracle,
the storyteller knew exactly what the lad had in mind.   She
stood on the corner with the late afternoon traffic whirling
past and repeated the "double talk" that comes at the end of
"Master of All Masters."   The youngster grinned, nodded his
head up and down, thanked her, and melted into the crowd.

Again, a young housewife and mother, being introduced
to a storyteller grown older, said, "Oh, I remember you!"
After a moment she continued, "I remember your voice.   You
used to tell stories at my school.   I'll never forget them."
A government official, asking help in the production of a television series for school children, stopped in the middle of an
interview and planning session, sat very still, and exclaimed,
"Now, I know who you are.   No wonder I wanted to do a series of programs on literature.   You were the one who told
stories to us.   It was you who helped me understand how nature influences people.   Come on.   You're just the person
we need to help put on this show!"

Storytellers sparkle as they tell how the friendly teas-
ing of technicians and camera men have changed to respectful
listening, as a structured radio or television story program
has progressed from a trial performance to a sustaining show.
All this is reminiscent of the child who skips down the hall,
away from story hour repeating bits of Millions of Cats. [2]

No storyteller need push for praise, nor should feel
a need to question a listener.   Hearing stories is an emo-
tional experience, and one's reaction is as personal, as pri-

vate as one's feeling about religion or love.   Sometimes listeners don't know what they think.   They may not feel they
are supposed to think anything at that moment.   They may
want time to mull over the sensation of a burgeoning imagination.   Was it not enough that a story was told and shared?

The apprentice storyteller should be encouraged to
imagine all the positive experiences a listener may receive
from a storytime.   Students should know there are several
benefits: listeners learn a new story (and are given a glimpse
of good literature), their perception of proportion is quickened,
their concept of the fitness of things is deepened, and perhaps
even they become more alert.   They may have had their first
lesson, via the plot, in sequential logic.   They may have
started to see the meanings of names of things, of people or
been encouraged toward more self-esteem.   Best of all is
when through stories the first steps are taken to identify oneself as a real person.   A true surge of happiness is possible
simply in being part of a group, in being, individually, one
with an adult--of being involved.

Although the signal purpose of the story remains entertainment, the listener may have come to realize that there
is good and evil; that it is a privilege to choose one or the
other.   Shakespeare's description of the casket scene in The
Merchant of Venice (Act II, Scene viii) had a lasting influence
on a high school student who said that until the moment she
read the scene she had wondered if there were any virtue in
choice.   A small child heard of this scene first from one who
told the tale from the Lambs' interpretation of the play.   That
child, when she grew up and went to Venice, could have no
peace until she relived the story of the play and walked on
the Rialto, imaging the several characters all about her.   She
thought once more of Belmont, wondering where it had been.

NOTES

1.   Clemens: p. 12.

2.   Gág.

Chapter Eight

THE GREAT DESIGNERS

In the National Gallery of Scotland in Edinburgh, there
is a painting by Chalmers entitled The Legend. This work
by a master chiaroscurist, employing a rich palette of browns,
greys, greens, and reds, portrays a spacious room with stone
walls and a low hearth with hints of a fire. Seated to the
left, in a chair carved from dark woods, is the storyteller.
Her left hand is extended in a slight gesture toward the eight
boys and girls grouped in a ragged crescent before her. One
child, propped by his arms, lies on the floor; a girl sits relaxed on a low stool.

The canvas depicts many aspects of the story experience, but only through suggestion can it reveal all the problems that faced the early designers of a return to this literary adventure for children, the story hour. Other than knowledge of the needs of boys and girls and an abundant enthusiasm,
these librarians had little with which to build. Few collections of stories for children were being published, and there
were few librarians trained to speak in public. On the other
hand, there were Andersen, the Grimm brothers, Jacobs,
Pyle, and Stockton. And there was Marie Shedlock.

The circumstances that led to the presence of Mary
Wright Plummer, director of the School of Library Science
at the Pratt Institute, Brooklyn, at a storytelling session presented by an Englishwoman, Marie L. Shedlock, in the elegant ballroom at Sherry's, in New York City, set the modern
course of storytelling in the United States. Shedlock found
avid listeners and learners among the teachers and librarians,
nation-wide, who heard her tell the fairy tales of Hans Christian Andersen and attended her classes in storytelling. They
made her welcome, and they kept her busy.

Mary Plummer invited Shedlock to Brooklyn and hear-

ing her there were two who could never forget: Anne Carroll
Moore and Anna Cogswell Tyler.   Although Moore was not a
storyteller, it was she who was to be the spark that lit the
story-hour candle for all time: she invited Marie Shedlock
to the Pratt Children's Room, and later to the New York Public Library; she appointed Tyler the New York Public's first
head of storytelling.

After Moore had heard Shedlock tell stories to children,
she knew that story hours must become a regular part of the
service to young borrowers. [1] She considered storytelling a
most important answer to youth's needs to share literature,
and she soon discovered that it could lead to friendships between adults and children.

Learning of Shedlock's visit to the United States, Alice
M. Jordan invited her to tell stories in Boston and arranged
for her to direct demonstrations and workshops. [2] As head
of children's services for the Boston Public Library, and later as book editor of The Horn Book Magazine, Jordan was,
at the turn of the century, already exploring new services for
children.   She possessed great vision and was perhaps the
first librarian to recognize the siren call of movies, and to
know that story hours should be as much fun as films in order to compete.

While Marie Shedlock contributed the pattern of what
should take place during a story hour--a carefully selected,
well-told story--and Moore added the air of festival and de-
lineated its purpose, it was Jordan who understood the need
for training storytellers who could establish regular programs.
Less than a decade after Shedlock's visit the Boston Public
was offering three superior storytellers to its young patrons.
They were Mrs. Mary Cronan, her husband, John Cronan,
and her sister, Mrs. Margaret Powers, and for thirty years
these three storytellers would influence the boys and girls
growing up in that city.

Sara Cone Bryant, [3] writer, anthologist, and storyteller, was also invited to Boston by Jordan in the early
1900's.   Bryant was adapting old folktales and writing, and
her How to Tell Stories to Children, published by Houghton
Mifflin in 1905, was perhaps the first book to give definite
instructions on how to proceed as a storyteller. [4]

Although Bryant's instructional work is no longer used
extensively, many of the stories she wrote and those she a-

dapted are preserved in collections and anthologies. Such
stories as "The Little Red Hen" and "The Gingerbread Boy"
were among her tales for the youngest listeners. She was
one of the first writers to suggest the importance of repetition in stories for children, the necessity to introduce a bit
of mystery, and the need for long stories to be edited for
brevity.

    Bryant's works were followed in 1915 by Marie Shed-
lock's The Art of the Story-teller, [5] which was to become the
most honored writing on traditional storytelling for many decades, influencing generations of storytellers. This book is a
compilation of her lectures, suggestions, and choice stories,
and includes a chapter containing questions teachers had asked
and the answers she gave. The third edition (see Bibliography)
is a greater and richer volume since it carries a Foreword
by Anne Carroll Moore, and "A New List of Stories" contributed by Eulalie Steinmetz Ross who was herself a librarian
and one of the truly great storytellers. Each selection included is proof of the faithfulness of Ross's desire and prom-
ise to include only those stories that Shedlock might have selected herself. These items reflect the skill of Ross and her
deep devotion to the storytelling ethic.

    Also in the list of early created aids for storytellers
are Anna Cogswell Tyler's Twenty-Four Unusual Stories and
Gardner and Ramsey's A Handbook of Children's Literature,
which was used as one of the first textbooks in courses in
children's literature and storytelling. Although the space devoted specifically to storytelling was minimal, the Handbook
authors explored the subject of "re-creative" storytelling.
They give credit to Miss A. J. Latham of Teachers College,
Columbia University, for having coined the phrase. [6] It may
also have been Latham who influenced Eloise Ramsey to rethink the value of memorizing material for story hours. It
is interesting to note that one of Ramsey's first students remembers that she required memorization in the preparation
of stories while one of her later students remembers that
she insisted on the use of the recreative method. This method,
still a favorite, stresses study of the story until mental pictures of the action, in sequence, can be formed and blended
with the rhythm of the author's style and language.

    Another of the earliest designers of storytelling was
Lucy Sprague Mitchell who was experimenting in New York
City with young children and their preferences in stories.
Mitchell's emphasis lay in the area of children's stories that

related to their small world: their bodies, toys, families, and friends. Her 1921 Here and Now Story Book, a collection of stories about this child's world, was to make a great impact upon both instructors and students in teacher-training institutions throughout the United States. In 1948 she revised the volume, noting that the changing world had caused her to refurbish her original volume and to update certain objects that appeared in the early life of a child.

Also prominent on the New York scene were Mary Gould Davis and Ruth Sawyer who were to become master storytellers. Their rich backgrounds in reading, travel, and folklore; their flawless skill in selection and powerful presentation set the highest standards for apprentice storytellers and inspired them to emulation.

Davis followed Anna Cogswell Tyler as supervisor of storytelling at the New York Public in 1922, and in 1930 published a collection of her own story-hour favorites, A Baker's Dozen.

Ruth Sawyer's The Way of the Storyteller was first released in 1942, and an enlarged edition was published in 1962. This volume, in either edition, is accorded by storytellers a reverence second only to that given Shedlock's famous old book by which it stands on the shelves of most libraries. Through her writings and her long ministry--perhaps the most compelling of any artist in the field of storytelling--she gave and still gives reassurance to storytellers who may be wavering in their loyalty to the traditionally told story in a world steeped in visual entertainment.

Sawyer also wrote award-winning fiction for children, and wrote and collected some of the choice stories being told today. It is hoped that with the rekindling of the oral tradition for children that the tales included in her book The Long Christmas will become more easily available.

The Midwest blazed its own trail early in the new century; the most active of these early notable storytellers were Gudrun Thorne-Thomsen, writer and storyteller from Norway, working first in the Chicago area and then in California; Carolyn Burnite in Cleveland, and Frances Jenkins Olcott and Edna Whiteman in Pittsburgh.

Thorne-Thomsen excelled as an educator, writer, lecturer, and storyteller. She still exerts great influence, more than twenty years after her death, upon storytellers through the magnificent recordings she made of some of her story presentations.

In Detroit, there was an especially enthusiastic group of storytellers. The Detroit Public Library's Children's Department, under the direction of first Elizabeth Knapp and then Jessie Tompkins, brought together librarians who had no other thought than that storytelling was one of the first rights and privileges of both children and children's librarians. Tompkins was an innovator: she saw the value of regularly scheduled story hours and she appreciated the need for the staff to be well-trained. Too, she saw early the need to offer experiences for her storytellers in various environments and sent them into the schools to tell stories. She made opportunities for them to learn the use of radio as a second storytelling medium. She also suggested, and supported, the first fumbling efforts in the creation of preschool story programs. The first story hour of this type was presented at the Francis Parkman Regional Library with Tompkins and Frances E. Burnside, the head of children's services there, as observers. Later, Tompkins supervised a more structured program that was to be most successful and replicated in many schools and libraries.

Like Anne Carroll Moore, Tompkins did not tell stories, but encouraged her staff to high levels of expertise in the art of selection and the skill and grace of presentation. She held meetings at which the librarians could listen to and learn from each other. While the librarians told stories, listened and learned, Tompkins studied them all! Newcomers were invited to tell specific tales, often from the folklore of their native areas. Among the storytellers in this gifted, experienced group were Burnside, Hazel Adams Richardson, Elizabeth B. Ulveling, Ruth Hoey, and Miriam Wessel. Through the years most of these librarians have continued to tell stories professionally and to be prominent as lecturers and instructors in this field.

In the far West Wilhelmina Harper, in Redwood City, California, was actively telling stories, serving as an administrative librarian, and collecting material for storytellers nationwide. Many of her collections, especially those prepared for use at holiday times, are still in print. The West Coast was splendidly represented also by Ella Young, who was from Ireland. Young was a superb storyteller and considered by many, as was Ruth Sawyer, "the storyteller's storyteller."

It was storytellers like Davis and Sawyer and Young who
through their gifts as folklorists, speakers, scholars, and
writers exemplified the best in the art, and through their
very devotion to and belief in the oral tradition were able to
entice others into this special profession.

Frances Clarke Sayers brought the world up-to-date
on Ella Young through her review of Young's autobiography,
The Flowering Dusk,[7] for The Horn Book Magazine, in May,
1945. In 1972, Sayers brought the world of storytelling in
touch with another of its earliest designers in the rich, personal biography, Anne Carroll Moore.

Not only with her writings does Sayers reinforce the
need for stories and storyteller, but through her own life as
a librarian, teacher, writer, and storyteller of wide experience and charm. In Summoned by Books, she underlines the
importance of purity, strength, scholarship, and purpose in
the art of the storyteller. She stresses the need for dedication in those who serve children, in her long-famous "Lose
Not the Nightingale,"[8] that was to librarians an irresistible
voice directing them not only to the choosing of the best in
children's literature, but to the best in all ramifications of
library work with the young: an instrument with which to
measure themselves as professionals and persons.

Storytelling is recognized by Frances Clarke Sayers
as the staunch ally of the good and the great in literature,
and she wrote that for the child who found it difficult to read,
storytelling gave an equal share in the literary heritage through
the spoken word; that storytelling is the means of taking the
books of first quality to a wider audience than those who might
find them on their own.[9] Sayers' belief that the essential
quality of childhood does not change should comfort and
strengthen today's would-be storytellers who are concerned
that the pressures of mass communication, comics, and television are draining away potential listeners. She reassures
them that for all the distractions there remains the mind of
the child, hungry for experiences and full of a sense of wonder.[10]

Also influential in training children's librarians and
storytellers in the West were Winifred Crosley in Michigan
and Elizabeth Burr in Wisconsin. Crosley was the producer
of the first important film on storytelling, "Art of Telling
Stories to Children."[11]

In the South, Nora Beust, professor of children's literature at the University of North Carolina, and later the first consultant for children's services at the national level, was among the first instructors in library schools to include lectures and laboratory periods in storytelling in the courses of study for children's librarians.

Anthologies and collections of stories also began to include some instruction in the art, and the growth and popularity of storytelling stimulated authors, and collectors, to prepare volumes of stories found to be successful.

Two folklorists who edited collections that became popular are Richard Chase and Sir Philip M. Sherlock. Chase published two volumes, The Jack Tales and Grandfather Tales, that were to influence preceptively the selection of stories for telling in the South for at least twenty-five years. These stories, discovered among the Southern mountain areas, especially North Carolina, were similar to the folktales of Europe. Since they were "homespun"--and those telling them were so charming using the native dialect and accent--it was difficult for instructors in storytelling to introduce what they considered purer versions of these old tales. While many teachers and librarians working near the counties where Chase explored will never be convinced, some storytellers are beginning to realize that there are other stories! One of the favorites among Chase's selections is "Sody Sallyraytus,"[12] and it has become popular in many regions of the United States.

Sir Philip M. Sherlock of Jamaica added to the Anansi tales his collection entitled Anansi, the Spider Man, West Indian versions of the doings of the wily African hero. Anansi, a favorite with authors and children, has appeared in many books in the past twenty years. One of the latest offerings is Carol Korty's Plays from African Folktales that offers four plays, two of which are about Anansi. Those storytellers who enjoy dramatizing stories with children will be helped by the author's suggestions and notes on costuming and special effects.

It was more than excellent writings, workshops, and formal classes in storytelling, however, that assured a renaissance in the art. The festival of stories held at Miami Beach during the American Library Association conference in June 1956 was one of the most significant events in the history of storytelling in the United States since the advent of Marie Shedlock. Master storytellers were honored with tales

told with special ceremonial grace. Stories written by Ruth
Sawyer and adaptations of Andersen, written by Shedlock,
were presented, and many librarians witnessed these occasions.

The event was important because of its purpose and
content, and for its celebration of the art. Too, it wrote the
final paragraphs of the first chapter of the modern story of
storytelling. The beginning era of the early designers had
closed: the challenge had been made.

At the festivities on Tuesday, June 19th, the day ded-
icated to Mary Gould Davis, the first storyteller introduced
was Augusta Baker. As she was presented some of the audience saw and heard, for the first time, the new leader-to-
be. Baker is perhaps the one greatest force in the further-
ance of storytelling throughout the country.

Augusta Baker is widely known as a master storyteller, and she is honored often for her artistry and leadership. She is a designer of workshops and lecture series; she
continues to write and to record, to inspire, and, gently to
remind those in authority to maintain and to enrich the story
experience. With children and parents demanding a return
of the oral tradition to schools and libraries, it is evident
that she has told her story well. She has kept the faith.

Others felt the need to speak up for storytelling and
to document its impressive history, and these writings gave
prominence to the beginning of the second chapter of the state
of the art. Starting the round of publications in the 1950's
was Charles Laughton with his article in the Atlantic Monthly.

In 1956 Gudrun Thorne-Thomsen wrote Storytelling and
Stories I Tell, and Jasmine Britton wrote in an article for
The Horn Book Magazine the story of this outstanding educator
and storyteller. Spencer Shaw wrote an article about his experimentation with stories and music, and in 1959, Ruth Tooze
published her book, Storytelling.

Each of these significant writings portrayed changes
and hinted at new trends: the passing of the great traditional
storytellers, beginnings of variations in the structured told-
tale, and the need for the emergence of additional leaders to
take the messages nation-wide.

Ruth Tooze did this through her teaching, lecturing,

and writings. She was a superb storyteller, and her art reflected her knowledge of children and young adults, her understanding of how children learn, her travels, and especially, her masterful use of the dramatic flair.

In North Carolina, even before Tooze went there to live, write, and lecture, Mary Peacock Douglas, supervisor of School Libraries in the Department of Public Instruction, well-known library administrator and library technologist, was encouraging librarians to place emphasis upon storytelling. She arranged for many special programs that brought popular authors and storytellers to her state. She also presented a specialist to introduce the value of radio-storytelling in taking folklore to a wide audience. Although she did not tell stories, she read to children and adults, and a favorite with her listeners was Something for the Medicine Man. [13]

Others in the South who influenced and enlarged the scope of storytelling as an institutional service were two library administrators: Mary Louise Rheay, director of Children's Services at the Atlanta Public Library, and Pauline Griffin, at the Department of Continuing Education at the University of Georgia in Athens. They offered teachers and librarians many opportunities to attend clinics, workshops, and tell-ins for storytellers.

The 1960's saw continued homage paid to the first great storytellers, and Ruth Sawyer was encouraged to restudy and enlarge her book, The Way of the Storyteller. One of the most valuable and practical essays on storytelling was written during this time by Eulalie Steinmetz Ross who included it as a carefully written postscript to her The Lost Half-Hour, a collection of story-hour favorites. Eileen Colwell, an English librarian-storyteller, published a pair of titles: A Storyteller's Choice and A Second Storyteller's Choice--each with helpful notes and instructions.

Elizabeth Hough Sechrist and Jeanne B. Hardendorft were still adding to their long lists of compilations (see Bibliography). Virginia Haviland's Ruth Sawyer was published in 1965, and continued the story of this gifted writer and teller of tales. Sawyer's My Spain: A Storyteller's Year of Collecting came in 1967.

In 1966 "The Pleasure Is Mutual," a film demonstrating the picture storybook program, was produced and created a renewed interest in sharing books with the young child.

Anne Izard, librarian-administrator-storyteller in Westchester
County, New York was featured, and her techniques were
highly influential through the country.

Although there was much experimentation through
multimedia programs centering around games, singing, and
puppetry, the oral tradition was still prominent among services for children.   Storytellers went also to rest homes and
club meetings, and were busy at holidays.   It was, however,
the blossoming of the picture book time, and more and more
young children were being given the lion's share of the librarians' attention.

With the late 1960's and '70's there appeared a wealth
of new material in Anne Pellowski's The World of Children's
Literature, May Hill Arbuthnot's Time for Old Magic, and a
new edition of the Anthology of Children's Literature.[14] Traditionalists were given reinforcement through the section on
"Storytelling" that appears as a part of the Appendix in this
latter volume.

Public libraries continued to structure and to sponsor
training sessions for storytellers, and classes in children's
literature allotted several days, or longer, to lectures on the
art.   Professional storytellers were invited to share their
stories and expertise.   Among the students were bright young
librarians-to-be who were well aware of the challenge of radio
and television to the storyteller.   One of these was Eleanor
Hawkins, who created the first commercial television story
program in North Carolina, for channel WFMY-TV, in Greensboro, around 1950.   Later, from New Bern in the same state,
she produced a similar program that has been continuously
popular for many years.

Two other leaders who encouraged storytelling and the
study of folklore were Diane Wolkstein working in New York
City and Gwenda Ledbetter in Asheville, North Carolina.
Wolkstein was making recordings, writing, and serving as a
storyteller, lecturer, and producer of a radio story hour.
She also appeared as keynote speaker for seminars on folklore and storytelling in various areas of the country.

Ledbetter is one of the true professionals: she is
tireless, willing to tell stories for hours, and her repertoire
is endless.   She worked with the children in Buncombe County
and appeared in a television series entitled "Tales from the
Red Rocker."   Completely at ease with both material and au-

dience, Ledbetter ranks with Davis and Sawyer in her mastery
of the art.

Her telling of "The Nightingale" by Andersen leaves
one with the clear sound of the silver bells in the emperor's
garden and the heavenly music of the bird as he sang in the
green woods.

It is surprising that the 1970's brought so few programs having stories central to their format to radio and television.   Equally unexpected, but cheering and reassuring,
was the large number of superior studies made and reported
in this decade.

One of the most helpful books on telling stories to
young children was a revision of Vardine Moore's Pre-School
Story Hour.   Zena Sutherland revised May Hill Arbuthnot's
... Anthology of Children's Literature,[15] and Sylvia Ziskind
published her Telling Stories to Children.   Sutherland also
brought out the fifth edition of Children and Books, and Caroline Feller Bauer produced her Handbook for Storytellers.
This volume considers many aspects of communicating with
children through books, and it is one of the few recent publications to discuss the use of mass media.

Together with Ellin Greene, Augusta Baker released
Storytelling, Art and Technique, and here one can find rem-
iniscences of the beginnings of storytelling in schools and libraries in the United States, a factual accounting of the second period in its history, and helpful suggestions for a successful continuance of the art.

With the publication of The World of Storytelling, Anne
Pellowski launched the third epoch of the art, skillfully bringing together the last pieces of the puzzle that have been elud-
ing folklorists and institutional storytellers for years: the
reconciliation of the many forms of folklore.   Her scholarly
and definitive work is a major contribution that can round out
the reading background of storytellers around the world.

By taking advantage of the rich resources created for
storytellers, other teachers and librarians have also helped
to fashion the dignified presentation and exchange of literature
with boys and girls through the art of storytelling.

The list of men and women who have created blissful
afternoons and evenings of sprites and spirits, talking ani-

mals and fairyfolk, is long, and often their art is unsung.
So, light the candles and declare festival for those who have
recognized the need of girls and boys to hear stories; to be
aware of the gripping literary heritage that is rightfully theirs.

NOTES

1.   Anne Carroll Moore: p. 145.

2.   Filstrup (see Articles section of Bibliography).

3.   Ibid.

4.   The 1924 edition published by Houghton Mifflin was
reprinted in 1973 by Gale of Detroit. Bryant's Stories to Tell
Children and Stories to Tell Littlest Ones were early collections also published by Houghton Mifflin.

5.   D. Appleton and Co.; Dover reprinted it in 1951.

6.   Gardner and Ramsey: p. 40.

7.   Ella Young, (Longmans) David McKay, 1945.

8.   Sayers, Summoned...: pp. 52-67.

9.   Ibid.

10.   Ibid., p. 112.

11.   See Films section of the Bibliography.

12.   Chase, Grandfather...: pp. 75-80.

13.   Hood.

14.   Johnson, Sickels, and Sayers.

15.   Arbuthnot.

Chapter Nine

THE FALLACY AND THE FANTASY

For all its prestigious history and innate elegance
storytelling probably should be presented to potential storytellers (in order to get their attention and support) as being
as easy as "A B C." Perhaps one could be tempted to say
that to maintain the nature and the spirit of the art is as
simple as the plot of "The Three Bears." The storyteller
will discover, however, that this particular nursery tale is
most complex. To recall, for telling, more than the basic
pattern is difficult without a quick look at the story itself.

This "simple" story should be easily found anywhere,
one supposes. The storyteller goes to a prominent listing of
good storybook titles with helpful notes and brief annotations.
Mildly amused, the searcher finds that also acceptable as the
title is "The Story of the Three Bears." One entry is reported as being "The Story of the Three Little Bears," but
further study of the volume in which this odd title is said to
occur shows that the title has been entered incorrectly. An
author-editor wouldn't use two titles for the same story--or
would she? More confusion is encountered when there is a
sprinkling of "see also's" but no "see's," and it becomes obvious that the editors have thrown up their hands. Decisions,
decisions.

One hastens to locate the various volumes containing
this tale--and one decides that, first, one selection from the
several versions must be chosen. Probably with surprise
the storyteller learns that Robert Southey is credited as the
author of the story. A folktale with one author? Many say
yes, and please, not to look too far to disprove the fact since
this poet laureate of England, who wrote so diligently for so
long--there are fourteen volumes of poetry and more to his
credit--is probably better known for writing "The Story of the
Three Bears" than for anything else he ever wrote--including

an excellent biography of Lord Nelson and the well-known
poem, "The Battle of Blenheim. "

The searcher, now at sea and doing battle, reads
somewhere that the Southey version is no longer used but that
it may be found in several well-known collections, and that
he is named as having written it.   But he didn't write it,
says yet newer information--not first, anyway.   With the ex-
plorer's curiosity and zeal, one forges on: to find that, no,
he never said he wrote it.   The malcontent then goes to the
honored source of Joseph Jacobs, [1] and learns that some of
the mystery has been cleared up.   But Jacobs has dug up a
second version that he includes in yet another collection of
English tales where he gives the story a new title, "Scrape-
foot. "

The plot quickens.   A fox has been substituted for
Southey's old naughty woman and the later American-English
Goldilocks, and now there is a third contender (besides Jacobs'
"Little, Small, Wee Bear") for the porridge.   This is more
like it.   Here is a real folktale: a beast tale--all animals,
pure and natural.   The teller/hunter now begins to sense
another fox--Reynard! Deeper and deeper into the woods of
folklore one goes: it seems now to be the Middle Ages, but
no.   One is precipitated into Oriental literature, then Aesop,
up through Chaucer (the old familiar borrower and friend),
himself.   One leaps ahead a few hundreds of years and finds
that the satirizing of society is involved; that the bears are
not always bears, but sometimes wolves; that the enemy is
really human, thieving, lying, and more than mischievous.

The monastic pen is put aside and then it is printing
which spreads the confusion.   The lion, cat, and badger are
introduced as victims or near-victims.   In 1250 a clerk named
Willem is supposed to have donated his skills to the story and
to have come up with a Flemish version.   Before this time,
however, in the twelfth century there is said to have been
Latin and German texts.   As early as the thirteenth century,
the French had produced the Roman de Renart.   This version
may have provided the basis for other European adaptations,
among which was Chaucer's "The Nun's Priest's Tale. " In
1481, William Caxton printed an English translation of a Flemish manuscript, and much later in 1919, John Masefield published his long poem, "Reynard the Fox," giving it a modern
treatment.

With this information spread out for perusal, one hears

a whisper of disbelief: a manuscript in the Osborne Collection of the Toronto Public Library, entitled "The Story of the
Three Bears," metrically related, with illustrations, had been
presented originally as a birthday gift to one Horace Broke,
September 26, 1831[2]--six years before Southey published his
account in the fourth volume of The Doctor. This new evidence casts some doubt on Southey's original authorship (which
he never claimed), but Jacobs wrote that a metrical version
by a "G. N.," introducing little "Silverhair," had been much
praised by Southey. So, one can hardly give Eleanor Mure,
the giver of the birthday gift, any more credit than Southey.

But all the storyteller wants in the first place is a
good telling of the story that could refresh the memory of a
favorite tale. A study of several versions (there are almost
as many as there are writers and storytellers involved with
this bit of folklore) leads the hunter through the change from
pots of porridge to bowls; from an old vixen of a woman to
a fox; from "Silverhair" to "Goldilocks"; through a variety of
sympathies, or lack of them, on the part of follow-up artists
and authors. To cut short the chase one would do well to
choose the telling by Flora Annie Steel.

It is disconcerting, however, to learn therein that there
was no "Mama Bear." The "middle-sized bear" is referred
as a male. L. Leslie Brooke came to the rescue in his 1934
The Story of the Three Bears, referring to the characters as
"Poppa Bear," "Momma Bear," and "Baby Bear."[3] Also,
Gruenberg twenty years later refers to the "middle-sized
bear's" porridge as being in "her" bowl. [4]

The folktale process is typified in the story of the Story
of the Three Bears. That tale's history is not yet complete.
Each storyteller may have to write a new version, but this
is the way it should be to exhibit, through individual creativ-
ity, true folktale development. Winner of the race the storyteller is not, but along the way some enlightening information
about Robert Southey has been uncovered, and, most glorious
of all, one feels rewarded for learning that Leonardo da Vinci
wrote fables: that he wrote of the fox, and that his fox was
clever; that Leonardo, using Aesop and other writers of the
earliest times, originated new beast tales by endowing the animals with human traits that matched those of the people in
his own life. Everyone should rejoice at learning that Robert
Southey wrote "Snips and snails and puppy dog tails...." He
also wrote "Sugar and spice and all things nice." Or did
he?[5]

As a folktale the story of the three bears and their sneak thief has firmly entrenched itself, and happily so, in the lives of countless millions. (Recently a poignant story appeared that demonstrates the influence of this nursery tale upon at least one very special child seeking security and love. 6) Studying its history as a story would seem to require a lifetime. As recently as 1976, Paul Galdone's The Three Bears created a new "Goldilocks" who is missing a front tooth.

Storytelling is many things, and its meanings and interpretations are as disparate as the personal discoveries and convictions of the blind men who touched the elephant. 7 Storytelling covers much ancient and modern literature as well as various media of presentation. It marries well with persons of all nationalities and all ages. It lives harmoniously with art and music. It is the companion of the writer, the composer, the actor, the puppeteer, and the public speaker. Interpretation, as well as definition, is as varied as all the persons who touch its world; its many facets have attracted their separate champions.

Storytelling embraces the past, present, and the future of all the races of earth. A story is real, it is fantasy, but its great stretches are sometimes fraught with fallacy. It often represents dilemmas; it harbors mistaken ideas. It is eternally changing.

Storytelling presupposes a central figure or figures, content/plot, a medium of communication, a speaker, and an audience. To talk of its utility is to denigrate the stature of a story; the meaning and influence of all folk-based tales can hardly be measured. An examination of the goals set by a central figure may elicit a treatise on the subject, but any attempt to bend a story, to attribute to it or its central character false virtues, is in itself unseemly.

One would do well to examine one's motives when it would seem that storytelling needs a defense or a reason for existing: beware the "use" of storytelling in the classroom or as a "stimulus" to "motor" responses à la the psychologists, or talk of its beneficence in a hospital. It meets needs through its very abstractions and limitless powers. A story is a reflection of the hearer him or herself; it just may be that because of its elusiveness and its impalpability, it can accomplish all it is often credited with; but to push it to those ends can be to mistreat it.

Structured programs involving tellable material do create salutary situations--but so do unstructured occasions.   Is
storytelling only palliative?   a narcotic?   an analgesic?   Is
it only grandparents, parents, and children?   Is it a means
of transmittal of a heritage?   Is it a folklorist telling anecdotes?   One sure question to be answered is, how well prepared may an individual be to accept and to enjoy his or her
verbal legacy?

All the facets of the oral tradition are brought into the
search for answers to these several questions--the storyteller,
the writer, the scholars, reference sources, collections of
materials and audiences.   It is comforting to know that the
heritage is being preserved by the caretakers of the art.   At
times when there are crises or a changing of lifestyles, any
source of pleasure, any avenue to identification with such a
cohesive power as a joint heritage, should be studied.   With
the value of the storytelling art beyond doubt, it should be re-
furbished by those in need of its power.

If indeed there has been a diminution in the United
States in the practice of the oral tradition, it behooves those
most closely associated with it to play their roles with greater
dedication.   The desire should be to increase not only the
storytellers' own personal skills but their commitments.   It
is true there has been a series of educational pressures that
have changed the nature of the traditional story hour in both
content and structure--as well as purpose.   While the art remains unblemished, its popularity has been questioned, and
practice of the art has decreased in schools and libraries.
Large numbers of people are being reached by some form of
story program, but there is a decided shift in the variety of
age levels in the audiences.   A greater number of young children than formerly are being offered experiences that combine
an introduction to printed materials with opportunities for
verbal and motor activities.

A return to a consideration in depth of the meaning and
the value of the art, and a rethinking of the total community
as audience (not only the very youngest child and the senior
citizen)--with equal opportunities for all would-be listeners--
would easily correct any discrimination that may be present
in the contemporary scheme.   A recognition of its true role
in culture transmission ought to place the told-story back in
perspective.

The community itself of course is central to storytelling. Actually, everyone practices his or her share of tale-telling: in stores, on the streets, in classes, in gatherings of all kinds, organized and otherwise.

Funds at several governmental levels represented in the local community are being allocated and spent to promote (in a small way, true) most of the arts, and schools and libraries contribute their expertise and support. Institutions of higher learning are affording facilities for continuing education and for lectureship series and there is governmental direction and supervision of many kinds of verbal communication. Bulletin board and newsletter space are provided and information such as lists of resource people and notices of opportunities for artists of all kinds are available in many locations in a community (the library, the high school, the college, city hall). The community needs only to be stimulated to greater effort--which should then be redoubled based on firsthand experience of the awe-inspiring returns on effort invested.

Writers, artists, and publishers are offering more and more sources for the study and selection of stories in the oral tradition. Colleges and universities are acquiring appropriate publications and professional collectors are busy bringing together various original documents for scholars who are still searching, comparing, and validating their finds.

Agencies created for educational and social services to children and adults--and churches and synagogues--are obvious sources of influence on a community's attunement to the value of the storytelling tradition. Centers of religious education serve as distributors of information; they provide a climate and a particularly valuable meeting place for the sharing of literature.

Free-lance storytellers and lecturers also influence the community, and are in turn shaped by it, for whatever their particular fields, their livelihoods generally come directly (or indirectly) from some governmental source, as do those of most teachers and librarians.

Colleges and universities not only serve as depositories for the precious books bearing the written tale, but they are primarily responsible for the professional training of storytellers: the continuation of the art so long delegated to the guilds in the neighborhoods of long ago. While colleges and universities were, and are, eager to bring together speakers on folklore and to provide occasions for the informal sharing of literature, it is possible that they have been remiss in another area of their responsibility to the oral tradition.

Their departments of speech and of graduate studies in education and library science have allowed the idea to grow that storytelling should not necessarily be a part of the courses of study for teachers and librarians. Boards of trustees should not be held responsible for their failure to consider storytelling a skill necessary to the job performance of teachers and librarians who work exclusively with children, but forgiveness cannot be meted out to faculties who are knowledgeable of the importance of the oral tradition and yet do not provide for its instruction.

Institutions of higher learning are however struggling nowadays to embrace the new worries created by changing times, and it is, sadly, possible that but few potential professionals in any field or discipline are currently receiving superior training.

Teachers and media specialists in public schools during the past twenty years have also been besieged by a series of circumstances that precluded their continuing to practice any gentle art regardless of their training or intuition. Fear of the scientific prowess of competing nations turned the attention of the United States toward science and research in technologies, not toward art and literature. Federal funds became available for library-related materials and some equipment, but only in a few instances did these funds cover hiring adequate personnel to administer the enhanced collections of audiovisual and other hardware items. It has been, therefore, difficult in the United States to maintain the degree of excellence desired in the fields for which these items were purchased. Media specialists were especially harassed, and they had to turn full attention to the writing of sci/tech-related project proposals, the perusal of new genres of catalog, and the acquisitioning of an endless list of paraphernalia (whose contents, or nature, often remained a mystery). There was little time for previewing or proper evaluation before selection; even less remained for such traditional librarianly duties as finding good stories.

Volunteers, acceptably trained or not, had to be welcomed, and later, inadequately-trained aides were pressed into service. The supervision of these willing helpers was time-consuming. The increase of preschool institutions such as day-care centers and kindergartens to care for children

whose parents were both in professions, business, or industry
added to the load of teachers and media specialists.   They
were now expected to perform miracles in supervisory roles
helping to train staffs, especially for agencies where children
of the ages from one to five were being cared for by government funds.

Not only was time at a premium, but the swift changes
in materials and the methods necessary to incorporate these
new articles into library routines called for a quick about-
face.   A shift in emphasis was forced from children to things,
and any attempt to acquaint children with their literary heritage seemed to be restricted to recorded, taped, canned, or
otherwise factory-made media.

Whatever effort that could be made by traditional storytellers began to be influenced by certain deleterious rumors:
story materials were difficult to come by, the learning process was long and hard.   It was bruited about that some selec-
tions--such as from Andersen, Kipling, Wilde, Stockton, and
Sandburg--were too precious to be told (unless memorized,
and this was discouraged)--that they should be read so
as not to lose any of the art of the writers.   The art
of these writers sustains itself.   It does not allow the
learner to want to omit singing phrases, perfect words.
These stories were meant to be told and in time anyone who
wants to can share them in this most traditional form.

Too, the method of committing these literary master-
pieces to memory was deemed fraught with the danger of forgetting.   It should be remembered that memorization is not
so difficult for the younger storytellers as it is for older
teachers and librarians.   Apprentices should not be discouraged in their planning to become familiar with these superior
stories.   Perhaps the frightening ingredient is the hard work
and not the fear of forgetting.   Should only the professional
actor and storyteller be encouraged to know the excitement
stimulated by these great writers?   There is an old saying,
"... how silent the woods if one could hear the songs of only
the sweetest singers. "

Too easily have these excuses risen to some lips, and
too easy is the defense of those loath to produce the beauty
of the told story.   Excuses for less and less of the formal
story exchange are found at the training level and in some
literature written on the subject of storytelling itself.   Writers in professional journals also have referred to the lack of

interest on the part of potential audiences. And again, television is often the scapegoat. If it is thought that television
is a greater attraction than listening to stories, that television
is excessively violent and base (and thus detrimental to the
child and the young adult), why are the efforts of training institutions not bent anew toward change? Instead, it would
seem that mere excuses are offered to some would-be apprentices and literary programs lessened in meaningfulness, to
others.

The training of teachers and librarians who will work
with children and their literary needs should include methods
and techniques in how to encourage boys and girls not only to
learn to read, but to understand the real meaning of the possession of such a skill, and to learn to enjoy the practice of
it.

Perhaps the greater emphasis and the lion's share of
the funds are misplaced. How one reads is important, but
so are that one reads and what. The storyteller influences
the skill and the quality, playing a significant role in encouraging the habit of going places where such reading materials
may be obtained easily, and free.

Excuses are quickly come by: the loss of clientele,
the difficulty of the art. These rascally rationalizations have
given birth to two cults of sharing literature with the young.
First, the media specialists and librarians who prefer the
variety programs say that these are structured to fit the needs
of the young child: to move, to speak, and to touch--to participate. These children are also being introduced to literature through recordings, filmstrips, and films. They are
learning to identify objects; to recognize colors; to know the
names of items prominent in their world. They are also becoming acquainted with the delights of music, verse, and
puppetry.

Traditionalists counter with what they believe to be
even more basic: an exercising of the imagination; the sensing of the enthusiasm and warmth of an adult who is relating
to a child on a personal basis through eye contact as well as
through the human voice, and its wide range of evocative
qualities.

Part of the variety program is the sharing of stories
through picture books. Here, however, the story is not so
important as the artistic interpretations. The barriers cast

by the book and its illustrations are cited as deterrents to
the close relationship desired--and evident--in the traditionalists' approach. The mechanics of the turning of the pages
and the maneuvers in order for all to see are obvious, and
there is little artistry in such a display.

The necessity for a child's being able to see a picture
of an object, together with the word (its name), was recognized in the middle of the seventeenth century when John
Amos Komensky--more familiar to librarians and students
as Comenius--published his Orbis Sensualium Pictus (or, just
Orbis Pictus). It is considered to be the first picture book
for children.

Illustrations aid in the identification of objects, but the
fallacy in the picture-book concept is that few children ever
really see anything. This type of program has greater impact when it is presented to only two or three children, and
they can actually see well enough to connect the words with
the illustrations, and are able to relate the one with the other.
If a book is shown to a group of more than three or four
children, at the most, they should be group-oriented enough
to consider the rights of each to view equally and to enjoy
the company of each other as much as the material being
displayed. When there are more than three or four youngsters, the use of multiple copies of the title, or an opaque
projector, should be considered.

The picture story program does not appear to be a
finished presentation. It is, to the traditionalist, only the
first step toward the mastery of a story, or book, by a storyteller who has decided to share a tale before experiencing a
oneness with a particular volume.

The picture book program had an honorable and altruistic beginning. It was first experimented with to show concern for the individual child. Through the offer to the child
of a feeling of closeness and friendship with the children's
librarian, it was hoped that even the youngest patron might
feel at home in the public library; to help these youngsters
to be aware of the increasingly large number of "two-laps"
books that were being published in the late 1930's. These
oversize picture books were excellent for sharing by the child
and an older person, with the librarian serving as catalyst to
facilitate, through demonstration, the acceptance of such an
activity in the home.

These books were also being introduced to small children to instruct them in the care and handling of library materials. As well, the books could assist the children in their assimilation of the fact that words are both spoken and printed: that printed words could be read aloud or silently; that they "said" the same message. The value in the sharing of a whole, physical book--illustrated or not--was supposed to lie in the demonstration that an adult enjoyed the process of reading--therefore a child should be pleased to imitate this action.

Primary grades in public schools employed picture books to show one way in which children could locate, on a page, words, generally nouns, and call their "names. "

The use of flannel or felt boards extended the illustrated type of presentation, and sometimes an available artist would take the place of both words and pictures through speaking and drawing the story at the same time. The flannel board approach made tangible--and of course more visible-- the persons and things written about in the story being portrayed. This method of sharing a story brought with it an element of suspense, and encouraged the centering of the children's attention on a fixed area. The flannel board also helped to involve the child in preparation of the materials used in telling the story.

Most of the flannel board presentations, however, are now conducted by adults, the boys and girls being kept around as "audience. " This type of program precludes the inclusion of older children unless they are brought into the group to serve as program assistants or as companions to young charges.

Other variety programs were brought to patrons in public libraries to acquaint children with the several forms of art: the drama, music, and puppetry. These special occasions did not take the place of the regular story hour. They were additions to any series previously scheduled, and were often included to cooperate with performers who wished both space and audience for their particular presentations. Some of these entertainments were productions by women's clubs, especially by organizations of young women who were active in community affairs, and in cultural interests and pursuits.

Sometimes the special programs consisted of only one person: a volunteer who wished to share travels abroad and would bring an exhibit of souvenirs; lecturers on subjects of

interest to children and youth.   Schools and libraries were in-
dulgent with these visitors, and as the number of resource
persons for such performances grew, the professionals in information centers began to realize how excellent these arrangements were for public relations and for enabling the release
of regular staff to go about their other duties.

The use of costumes, as well as realia, suffered a
sea change from the ball gown of the elocutionist.   Native
costumes of a country visited by a lecturer made their appearance along with the other remembrances brought back
home.   Guest storytellers would display small objects to illustrate their stories: a set of wood carvings, a collection
of dolls, or shells.   As the sophistication of the returned
traveler grew, the collections changed to slides and films to
illustrate vacations at home and abroad.

These programs were interspersed with anecdotes,
and they lent variety and color to the sometime prosaic services to the young.   These occasions were well attended, and
soon they began to supersede the oldfashioned story hour.

The introduction of films, many and excellent, produced especially for young audiences, was a telling blow to
the told story.   Girls and boys, during the period when films
were first coming into prominence, were so at home with
television, and films, that they could be amused without the
expense of much energy on the part of anyone concerned.
Thus, the intimacy and the stretching of the imagination that
went along with a tale's being spun by some enthusiastic adult
was lost, for the time being, in many schools and libraries.

A series of popular filmstrips were also used by libraries whose children's services staffs were too small (or
non-existent) to mount a viable story hour.   The age level
of the audiences, in libraries, began either to drop or to
elevate: young children for picture-book and variety programs,
older boys and girls for book talks and film showings, and
lectures for adults.

The uses of picture books and other devices lowered
the personal contact between the performer and the group,
and the special benefits accruing from the age-old manner of
sharing the folk heritage were diminished.   Caroline Bauer,
in her Handbook for Storytellers, records most of the known
combinations of devices, and supplies the reader with many
of her own inventions and creations.   For builders of such
variety programs, her book is exceptionally helpful.

Traditionalists do not employ any kind of device since they believe that youngsters are distracted by the various articles and activities. From their own experiences they know that even quite young children can relate easily to a told story. They also believe that the human voice is adequate to create a tale so complete that children can call up for themselves unbroken sequences of mental pictures of both characters and action.

Any storyteller, however, has to have a bag of tricks, but the traditionalists prefer to use mimicry, interpolation, and pantomime to denote such varieties and changes in the tale, as it unfolds, that are thought expedient and necessary for clarification. Whether or not one uses devices, according to Charlotte Huck[8] and others, it is the sincerity and the enthusiasm of the speaker that pleases and holds the interest of one's audience.

Regardless of the puristic feelings of the traditionalists, there must be opportunities somewhere for boys and girls, the younger the better, to experience the beauties of all the arts, especially of music and sculpture. Whether or not this responsibility is the storyteller's is still questioned.

Public school laws require that teaching faculties possess expertise in certain of the arts, but beyond some knowledge of folk material, storytelling does not appear to be one of them. This art is left too often to the media specialist who is, even in the most felicitous situations, more than overburdened with the many duties of an information center. As schools strive to incorporate new disciplines, new methods, advanced technologies and concepts, it is to be wondered whether or not school librarians and media specialists should be considered, at the present time, as possible transmitters of the folktale.

The children's librarian, perhaps, is the proper professional, being familiar both with children and with literature. The responsibility of the librarian who works with boys and girls is not only to introduce children to books and materials, but to aid in their interpretation. While it is impossible for the staff working with children and youth to tell all the stories or plan all the programs (however good an idea this would be in the ideal) the public library should make itself available as a clearing house and as an impetus for the provision of these services.

The public library sometimes forgets that the two main purposes for having a program for children are the children and their literature. All too obviously faulty in regard to whom should the children's room serve is the thinking behind one state bureaucrat's written job description of the duties of a professional children's librarian that included, as the first item, "... the interpretation of children's literature to adults."

The role of the children's room staff is to think Children. When there is no doubt that the staff considers this the overriding concern, all responsibilities, efforts, and judgments tend to fall neatly into place. The story hour becomes one of the services that offers time for personal communication with all the children and with the best material in the collection.

Librarians planning to work with children and youth should expect--demand, if necessary--to receive training in storytelling from the professional schools. Excoriation of persons or institutions that do not offer such an opportunity should not be indulged in, but failure to meet this need should be brought to the attention of those who could remedy the situation.

Adults as well as children enjoy the release and the relaxation of time spent with the fairy and folk element. Recall the fascination, long years after children had welcomed Bilbo Baggins, of young adults, then adults, with Tolkien. The popularity of television series such as Bewitched and I Dream of Jeanie is witness to this need.

The trend back to the oral tradition is encouraging, and new children's librarians are requesting classes in the art of storytelling. Universities are arranging for seminars that are open to anyone qualifying for their programs in continuing education. Children, too, are stirring in this direction. When they were young they enjoyed the variety programs in schools and libraries, and as they grow older they do not want to be bypassed in order for the next generation of little ones to receive all the attention and the fun and games.

It is the new (young or old) potential storytellers who will prove to be the staunchest supporters of the return of the traditional story hour. Their interest and concern, and determination, should be able to break the spell of the rumors "that storytelling is too hard, too time-consuming, not attractive enough to hold the attention of today's child."

NOTES

1.   Jacobs: pp. 254-255.

2.   Johnson et al. :   p. 183.

3.   Children's Catalog, 11th ed. H. W. Wilson Co. ,
1966; p. 76.

4.   Gruenberg: p. 274.

5.   Christopher Morley, ed. , Familiar Quotations,
12th ed. , rev. & enl. , Little, Brown, c1948; p. 322.

6.   Sachs.

7.   Quigley.

8.   Huck and Young: p. 388.

Chapter Ten

"AND GLADLY WOLDE HE LERNE..."

One of the joys of being a storyteller--perhaps the
greatest--is the realization that reading, study, practice, and
the sharing of one's finds in literature result in personal
growth.

This knowledge comes only after a period of true dedication, but it comes. One awakens to find new wealth: a
feeling of solid worth, a sense of accomplishment. While the
understanding of it all comes slowly, it stimulates, directs,
and encourages storytellers to continue to improve their skills;
to reach out for new exciting techniques; to initiate projects
in research. This growth compels one to continue to keep
pace with the art.

Storytellers should evaluate their methods of learning
by examining past programs and performances in an effort
to refine style and to enliven presentations. One must look
around for different materials and, to keep up, study new
catalogs, read recent publications, and define relationships
between the old and the new titles. One should constantly be
assessing (when possible) the better of two stories, two books,
two poems. In this revaluation, there should be no fear that
the old may appear drab. The good will remain so; the less
than best should be discarded. New collections and anthol-
ogies--as well as essays concerning changing trends in literature for children and youth--must be analyzed, always in
comparison with the storyteller's own experiences with what
has been found acceptable before.

Some storytellers may want to consider a change in
audiences. If one has been telling stories primarily to children, one may choose to work with young adults. When one
has been accustomed to small groups, carefully controlled and
regimented, it may be refreshing to experiment with a totally
voluntary assembly of listeners.

Whatever changes may be contemplated, one may begin
by studying one's past career.   It is important to ferret out
any weaknesses and identify one's mistakes.   Not to be overlooked is setting up ways to refine what is already good in
one's presentation.   Central to this self-improvement should
be a familiarity with what is being published and reviewed.

A visit to the shelves of a well-stocked library that
has kept up with publications in the fields of children's library services, folklore, and storytelling yields many volumes
to be taken down and studied.   Find again Virginia A. Tashjian's Juba This and Juba That, Elsie Ziegler's Folklore,
Margaret Bradford Boni's Fireside Book of Folk Songs, Ann
Cole's I Saw a Purple Cow, and Virginia Haviland's The Fairy
Tale Treasury.   Become acquainted with John E. Brewton's
Index to Children's Poetry, Norma Olin Ireland's Index to
Fairy Tales, Meigs' A Critical History of Children's Literature, Jean Karl's From Childhood to Childhood, and Patricia
Cianciolo's Illustrations in Children's Books.   Each of these
books is superior in its field, representing careful thought,
accurate presentation, and the highest of purposes.

Three publications that should become a part of the
personal libraries of storytellers are: Katharine Briggs' An
Encyclopedia of Fairies..., Robin Palmer's A Dictionary of
Mythical Places, and Ruth W. Gregory's Anniversaries and
Holidays.   Two other titles published by the American Li-
brary Association besides Gregory's important tool, are the
Subject Index to Poetry...[1] and Rufsvold's Guides to Educa-
tional Media.

The beginning storyteller may be overwhelmed by a
long list of resource materials, but will soon see the wisdom
in keeping up with the best thought, creative ideas, and the
latest editions of reference books in the many associated
fields of interest that overlie the province of the storyteller.

Together with reading and study, the apprentice may
want to do a bit of experimenting.   One children's librarian
began with the rhyming of stories, and she found that this
activity opened up a whole new world.   Poems that tell stories, especially, if they can be kept short, may be slipped
into a program to serve as openers, breathers, or the salient
parts!   The storyteller turned jingler does not want to change
wording, and the story must not be altered too radically, even
to fit a rhyming pattern.   One favorite to work with is Hope
Newell's The Little Old Woman Who Used Her Head.   Written

in what a storyteller named "anapestic mixturemeter," the
story-poem has been told with a deal of success.   A second,
"Christmas on Big Rattle,"[2] originally published in the Youth's
Companion, 14 December 1905, and written by Theodore Good-
ridge Roberts, was also turned into verses that seemed to add
pleasure for the listeners to the story of Archer and Sacobie
Bear, the Micmac Indian who had a unique method of exchang-
ing holiday gifts.

Storytellers may turn to the learning of a new language,
trying their hands at translating well-known stories, or learning to tell a folktale in its original language.   If he or she is
to face groups of Spanish-speaking children repeatedly, a storyteller will definitely begin to wish for this added skill.   Before a group of students who know a smattering of French,
Frances Steegmuller's Le Hibou et La Poussiquette would be
excellent fun.

Storytellers may broaden their interests through trying
to write some stories for telling.   With increased opportunities for study and travel, one's adventures may be turned
into fiction, travel sketches, or new versions of folktales
heard along the way.   Too, when storytellers have difficulty
in finding exactly what they want for a special occasion, they
may be further stimulated to create something on their own.
A close association with folklore and short stories makes this
work easier, although it is not necessary to mount a detailed
study of folktales to progress in one's art.

When a storyteller is a member of a professional staff,
however, making oneself available to help answer questions
that fall into this area is most rewarding.   Pursuit of factual
information relative to salient points in the history of a tale
whets one's appetite.   While this work may become time-
consuming, storytellers learn bits and pieces that flesh out
their backgrounds.

During such an experience, a storyteller discovered
new information about Hans Christian Andersen.   Sources of
his tales had never been studied since it was assumed that
the stories were original.   Most of Andersen's fairy tales
are, but the story being studied, "The Emperor's New Clothes,"
which is among his first published tales, was not.   The story
was taken from the writings of Prince Don Juan Manuel of
Spain, and the source was noted by Andersen, himself, in
his Preface, 1837: for the Older Readers.   Andersen wrote:
"For the whole amusing idea we must thank Prince Don Juan

Manuel, who was born in 1277 and died in 1347. "[3]   Andersen's retelling was published first in a booklet that also included "The Little Mermaid," and the year was 1837, evidently the same year the first hardbound book of the first stories was released. [4]

Once new facts are discovered and become part of the storyteller's background, interest is heightened; the telling more personal and authoritative.   A study of this same set of notes by the Danish writer could lead to further consideration of In Spain, a travel book published in 1836, and reputed to be one of the most successful books for adults.   One can easily imagine how a storyteller or a writer could be led on and on.

Andersen was not alone in his borrowing.   Giovanni Boccaccio (1313-1375) selected old folktales from the French and Oriental languages for The Decameron, which appeared in 1348-53.   It consisted of one hundred short stories told by ten young aristocrats fleeing the plague and going to Florence.   In this setting Boccaccio felt quite at home since his family villa was located there.

Undoubtedly, Geoffrey Chaucer borrowed from Boccaccio the lazy, storytelling-structure to set forth The Canterbury Tales, completed sometime between 1386 and 1400, the year of his death.   Turn-about being fair play, Boccaccio borrowed from Chaucer whose work was known to him, and whom he may have met when the English poet travelled to Italy on a diplomatic mission from 1372-1374.   Chaucer borrowed from Dante and Petrarch.   Petrarch was a friend of Boccaccio, and the Italian storyteller-writer is considered the first biographer of Dante--so it goes.   What a wonderfully small but marvelous world this is.   Imagine the "tellin" that could have been enjoyed by these great storytellers if they were fortunate enough to have met and known each other, and to have swapped stories.

William Shakespeare, of course, was a great borrower --perhaps the most famous of them all.   He took ideas and plots from Raphael Holinshed's Chronicles, from Sir Philip Sidney, Edmund Spenser, Thomas Lodge, Giraldi Cinthio (for the germ of Othello), and it is well-known that he was quite aware of both Chaucer and Boccaccio as well.   Hundreds of authors were his benefactors, but his great genius made their works his own.

However important uncovering these facts may be, storytellers could make more significant contributions through studies of the research done in the area of storytelling itself and, when little is found, to press for more. A definitive study of central-city kids and their needs for story programs would not fail to interest those who are able to provide opportunities for this type of research. Statistical studies, for those who felt capable, would bring to light the paucity of offerings in the oral tradition for the child of the inner-city who would benefit much from such programs.

Sharing literature with persons of a large city can be an adventure in itself. A storyteller once went into an almost forgotten spot in a metropolitan area to tell stories. Since it was a mercilessly warm day, and she had arrived early, she wandered into a tiny shop across the street from her destination. A cold drink would be refreshing, she thought, and she stepped inside the door to purchase one. For a moment it seemed there was no one inside, but after a short time, as if by magic, a large portion of a wall took shape and began to move toward her. The shape lost its squareness, and it became a huge man in dark clothes, topped by a thick sweater, open and showing a white shirt underneath. Startled by the size of the man, and by the fact that he wore such a thick sweater in almost a hundred degrees' temperature, she hesitated, said it was hot, and she would like a cold drink, please. As she started to the wooden ice chest to serve herself, the man began to rail at her in a hoarse scream.

"You'd better thank your Maker that it's hot! It's the cold that's cruel--cruel! But you wouldn't know what it is to be cold." With that remark he began to pull at his clothes, unbuttoning his shirt, exposing his bared chest and abdomen. The storyteller, mesmerized, watched as he displayed a great band of black across his belly; testament to his experience with crippling cold.

"See that," he demanded, jabbing his fingers toward his middle, "see that?" He drew out a chilled, dripping glass bottle of soda, wiped it dry, opened it, and handed it to her. "That's what," he said, pointing again to his evidence, "that's what it means to know cold."

Controlled now, and less afraid, the storyteller made appropriate, comforting remarks about his scars, and sat

down, from raw emotion, upon the edge of the chest.   Then,
the real story came.   The storekeeper had been a member
of a platoon that had been sent--and forgotten--to Russia during the First World War.   Since the men were considered
dead, from exposure, they were not searched for, and were
not found until long after they had lived through many months
(years, according to the raconteur) of severe privations.   The
chilling details poured forth, and the listener evidently reacted
right; the drink ended up as a gift.   The greater present,
however, was the story itself, sending the young storyteller
to her public library.

The story was found to be true, every word, and when
she learned that a monument had been placed to the dead of
this gallant group, she made a pilgrimage to the city ceme-
tery.   There was the great white bear: a statue standing
tall to the memory of her host and his comrades.   Bravery,
a fear of the cold, a love for the art of the story had all
been evident in his tale--and the mystery of the phrase, "Do
you know the Bear?" the man had repeated over and over
again, was solved.   While in the shop, she could call to mind
nothing but a restaurant that was so named.   Now, she understood.

Another personal experience that impressed a storyteller, making her aware of changes and additions that could
be incorporated into storytelling, was whispered in a spoken
desire to learn to play a guitar.   She had heard an almost
wraith-like girl, all in white, play and sing her strange folksongs, sitting on the walk that leads up to the campus at
Berkeley.

Many of the hurrying, noonday crowd of students stopped
to listen; some paused only long enough to toss coins into the
small basket at the girl's feet.   She, herself, felt so completely caught up into this re-enactment of ancient minstrelsy
that she knew at once she wanted to add a musical accompaniment to some of her own story presentations.

Many storytellers learn puppetry, augmenting their
stories by a combination of plot, painted fist-faces, strings,
and illusion.   For the inventive storyteller, opportunities to
expend one's energies are myriad.   During a ban on the use
of certain musical selections controlled by the American Society of Composers, Authors, Publishers (ASCAP), a producer of a radio program was faced with no available background music for a program that was to feature the story,

"Shen of the Sea."[5] Turning from the book, the storyteller went to the piano, picking out what was hoped would be mistaken, not only for music, but for <u>Chinese</u> music. The combination of minor chords and dissonants sounded similar only to a poorly, but more slowly, played "Chopsticks."

Thus, presentations may grow from one story to a program that includes poems, short tales, a bit of music, or some original contribution by the storyteller. As storytellers grow in skill, the audiences become more attuned to the charm of the speaker and the art. A group is eager to sit and listen, held through sheer magic woven by the combination of words and the eyes and voice of the storyteller, as the bear once was held by the shepherd boy's blue eyes![6]

When storytellers begin to feel a need for adding brief storytelling poems, they could hardly do better than to turn to the Brewtons and their collections. One of these excellent volumes is <u>Bridled with Rainbows</u>. Rachel Field is represented here, and one of her poems included is "Roads."[7] It is near-perfect to set a mood for going anywhere (or to fairyland), but the familiar is turned into mystery as the poet describes where roads may lead. Another from Field is "Something Told the Wild Geese,"[8] and again, the poet makes a pleasing combination of beauty in nature and the inimitable instincts of the bird kingdom.

For the very young, the poems of Marie Louise Allen, "The Mitten Song" and "My Zipper Suit"[9] have delighted thousands of children and have also facilitated their interest in clothes, learning to call these garments by name and knowing how to take them off and to put them on again. It is crude, perhaps, to put poems to such menial tasks, but then sometimes utilitarian uses must be made of material that can well stand the strain and stress of kindergartners. Rhoda W. Bacmeister's "Galoshes"[10] is the perfect partner for mittens and zipper suits. "Pockets" by Susan Adger Williams[11] expresses a less mundane use of those important appurtenances, but the poem is delightfully child-like and easily reminiscent of "The Princess Whom Nobody Could Silence,"[12] and Dr. Seuss's (i.e., Theodor Geisel's) <u>And to Think That I Saw It on Mulberry Street</u>. Boots and Marco are friends anybody would exchange pockets with, any day.

Valine Hobbs' "One Day When We Went Walking" and "The Grocer and the Gold-Fish" by Wilfrid Thorley[13] are unsurpassed as clever, modern, universal delicacies. Imagin-

ation and humor and everyday experiences are all rolled up,
snuggly, to become anything a young mind can dream up.

For older listeners, there are three poems storytellers
have used with success for many years: Mildred Plew Meigs'
"The Pirate Don Durk of Dowdee," Robert Southey's "The
Inchcape Rock," and Ruth Sawyer's translation of "Words from
an Old Spanish Carol." These poems set entirely different
moods, and are very effective when placed with other appropriate material. The richest gift storytellers can offer, however, is when they no longer need to seek the rhymed verse
of others; when their art in combining words and voice makes
its own poetry.

Sometimes at the cresting of a storyteller's career,
comes the desire to find and share a perfect story--to come
upon a piece of writing so delicate, so sensitive that it can
express all the emotions experienced during the long years of
work, the energy expended in learning to clear away the mechanics of the art. The storyteller reaches out to stories
that have been held in awe, perhaps thought to be beyond
ordinary capabilities. The storyteller needs the assurance
that this feeling comes to many, and that the final push may
be a particularly promising audience, or an obsessive desire
to stretch oneself.

Andersen's "The Nightingale" is one of the first such
stories the trembling artist may consider. A second is an
adaptation of sequences in Valenti Angelo's Nino; a third,
parts of Elizabeth Coatsworth's The Cat Who Went to Heaven.
Nino is made of the smells and textures, and the longings,
of an artist; from the clarity of a child's remembering, and
of his loving; from his sense of wonder. In The Cat Who
Went to Heaven, again, nature, art, and aspirations are a-
bundant. The special nature of these stories and books, and
others like them, has brought them together, and a new cate-
gory, "the art story," has developed logically.

Do not mistake the word "art" as signifying that all
the stories in such a group must be about art or should have
been written by artists, real or fictional. One of the most
vigorous of all selections chosen for special occasions is the
fiery, almost belligerent story dealing with the supernatural,
the winds of heaven screeching around the corners, and the
mighty voice of a great American sounding above it all.
Stephen Vincent Benét has fashioned in "The Devil and Daniel
Webster" a tale calling for the whole range of skills of a

storyteller. The author pulls all the stops in an organ to describe this magnificence--diapason fully extended. The viril-
ity of the early Colonial citizen, his determination to survive
and to contribute to his newly-freed country are evident. His
battle is not against the English; it is against evil--the very
devil himself.

A much calmer, but uniquely stirring story, is "The
Golden Parrot." Here, one also finds color and atmosphere.
There are other excellent tales in Three Golden Oranges,[14]
but this one is certainly the most beautiful. De Maupassant's
"The Piece of String" demonstrates the world's haste to judge,
to plague, to refuse to listen. It is a most compelling story,
demanding mastery. One finds a similar theme, for children,
in Eleanor Estes' The Hundred Dresses.

Rudyard Kipling writes in "The King's Ankus" of the
folly of man's drive for riches; finding death instead. In
"The Cat That Walked by Himself," Kipling, like Aesop, has
chosen an animal to play the role of self-reliance, and set
him in the dignity that belongs to the wilds. Great love and
tenderness are the themes of the two Oscar Wilde stories that
many storytellers want to share: "The Happy Prince" and
"The Selfish Giant."

Another favorite is Frances Frost's adaptation of Gian
Carlo Menotti's libretto for his opera "Amahl and the Night
Visitors." A second poetic child, fascinating to the storyteller, is Calpurnia, the main character in Rawlings' The
Secret River. She portrays all of childhood: light-heart,
perseverance, determination, fear; with all its yearnings and
its beauty. Imagination is the theme of the sequences ex-
hibiting Calpurnia's fears, and this wisp of humanity is hard
to catch in a telling, but finally, she stands still for the
storyteller, allowing her poetry to be repeated.

These are only a few of the art stories that wait to
be discovered, but finding oneself within their spell, the
storyteller comes to realize how great is the magic of words;
how penetrating the authors' humanity. One does well to seek
new dimensions. How else can storytellers reawaken the
hunger for roots and heritage, and then minister to it?

NOTES

1. Smith and Andrews.

2. Dickinson and Skinner: pp. 329-335.

3. Andersen: p. 1069.

4. Ibid.: p. 1072.

5. Chrisman: pp. 29-41.

6. Shedlock: p. 184.

7. Brewton and Brewton: p. 3.

8. Ibid.: p. 107.

9. Ibid.: p. 19, p. 20.

10. Ibid.: p. 24. First published in Bacmeister's Stories to Begin On, E. P. Dutton, c1940.

11. Ibid.: p. 26.

12. Hutchinson: pp. 125-133.

13. Brewton and Brewton: p. 29, p. 73.

14. Boggs and Davis.

Chapter Eleven

EXPANDING ONE'S AUDIENCE

Many institutional storytellers, especially children's librarians, begin their careers in the art by arranging a variety of entertainment for young children.   They inherit a fixed pattern of sharing the oral tradition and, with little training and insufficient experience, they willingly slip into place in an existing program.   They accept and conform to policies, continuing to implement plans similar to past efforts.   Materials are plentiful; audiences are readily available, and the new staff members are eager to begin.

Young children must be entertained rigorously and well in order that they may stretch their interest span, but this cannot take place until they learn to listen.   The librarian, teacher, or volunteer must accept and fulfill this two-edged responsibility.   Storytellers are wise to observe carefully the first group of youngsters with whom they meet.   Appraisal of the reactions of these children will give insights that can influence and guide methods adopted in the future.

One will find that sound filmstrips, and films with few words and much action are good for a start.   Films that show real children doing projects with clay, boxes, drawing, and playing have been found to hold the interest of even the youngest child.   Some excellent ones are available, and they should be ordered for previewing whether or not they are finally marked for purchase.

The learning period for a child to begin to listen should not be over-long, and the storyteller will want to include a short, told story in each session.   With "stage properties" kept to a minimum, listening to a story helps to develop the child as a thinking participant in the story hour. These thinking exercises are a welcome change from the types of activities enjoyed at home, in play schools, and in other institutions.

From experiences during a story hour, the young child
is becoming accustomed to being a member of a group, and
to sharing an occasion with an adult other than one who is
known through family or neighborhood ties.

Telling stories to young children is more difficult than
sharing a tale with older boys and girls, or adults, because
selections must be very carefully chosen.   Material should
be governed by the prospective audience: its degree of sophistication, its experiences in listening, and its interests.   The
purpose and length of the individual program, as well as the
storyteller's abilities and preferences, also influence selection.   The concentration of the age factor delimits the search
for literature to be shared, and in some ways prohibits its
being presented in a traditional manner.

Programs for young children are generally held in a
library during the morning hours.   They should not be allowed
to interfere with after-school activities for older boys and
girls.   Saturdays, in most areas, should be eliminated, and
Sundays may be carefully examined as times for special family programs.

The time of day, and the day of the week, must be determined early in the planning.   A brief study or a simple
survey should be undertaken.   By no means should staff preferences be allowed to set the time.   If a program for children is to be successful, it should be arranged with more in
mind than whether or not a storyteller finds the time convenient.   An adequately-qualified and interested person will be
glad to conform to the appropriate decision.   Primary and
play-school teachers are free to select almost any time when
the children may be ready to listen.

Other plans are similar to those for any story hour,
but special care must be taken to furnish the correct publicity.   Announcements spoken from church pulpits probably
reach more ears than any other method of communication
available to those wishing to extend an invitation to this special audience.   A second sure and safe method is to place
signs or posters near a cash register in a supermarket.   Notices in newspapers will be read by some; public service announcements by radio and television help.   Word of mouth is
dependable, but a sign in a public library is one of the least
successful ways of acquainting most parents of young children
with news of a prospective story hour.   Much effort is wasted
when only a small number appear to share a carefully planned

event, and the loss sustained by those who miss out on the fun is inestimable.

Another problem calling for satisfactory resolution is the handling of adults who accompany the young audience. When adults are allowed to remain with the children they have escorted, space is the important item to be considered. In the past, storytellers have gone to a great deal of trouble to separate adults from their charges. This action necessitates the arranging of an additional in-house program or leaves the sponsoring agency responsible for the children when the story hour has been concluded. It is most unwise to allow a program for young children to deteriorate into release-time for parents, teachers, or nannies. Inclusion of the adults in the festivities is strongly advised since this would accomplish a first important step in the growth and development of the storyteller in coping with a mixed group of listeners.

A storyteller would find that writing down a few points relative to the planning of story hours for young children is helpful, and, in summary, it could look something like this:

STORY PROGRAMS FOR YOUNG CHILDREN

Time: A midweek morning, about ten o'clock; on a nine-month schedule at least but preferably year round; to last no longer than thirty minutes. Extra time may be allowed for circulation of books after story hour. (No attempt should be made to work around local kindergarten schedules that complicate an otherwise acceptable arrangement.) Seek an audience not already over-involved.

Audience: Fifteen or twenty children; more if there is space; with or without adult companions. Irregular attendees always welcome. Never refuse a child who is in the library and wishes to participate.

Parents and Adults: Some type of program may be arranged by another staff member, for adults accompanying children, if this is possible and desired. Suggest adults remain with group, not necessarily with own child. Children enjoy seeing adults enjoying the stories.

Registration: Prior registration should be done only to ascertain the need for a second, or other, series. These programs may utilize similar material, or they may be an entirely different type of activity. If there is a registration, of value would be an alphabetic list of names, ages, parents' and guardians' names and addresses, telephone numbers at home and work, and other pertinent information (such as physical handicaps that could require adult assistance). If there are to be trips or excursions outside the library, a signed permission from the appropriate adult should be on file with the institution in charge of the tour.

Publicity: Adequate, correct, and consistent. News stories to announce introduction of new and different series of programs, or significant changes in ongoing ones. Coverage requested by the news media should be welcomed if policies allow. Representatives of various other institutions and agencies serving children may be invited for visits. Posters and signs in supermarkets, public health centers, social services offices, and in synagogues and churches.

Materials: A permanent, always available, collection of books, anthologies, and volumes of single stories for learning, for referral and study. Additional copies should be ready for circulation. Books on storytelling and variety programs for children should be included.

Program: Several short, carefully-selected stories should be prepared although only one or two may be told. They are essential to establish mood or to fit in with an already established one; be flexible. The shortest, best story should be told first to explore prevailing temperaments. Arrange opening ceremony if desired; story-hour symbols: bell, soft and mystical; candle, to be lit and to burn throughout program, to be extinguished with wish; the sounding of a gong: all are exciting and help prepare for fun and festival. Other objects may be chosen. Select opening phrases carefully; have own "signature" if appropriate. A good-morning puppet, or any attractive attention-attractors are fine.

Program Variations: Some storytellers feel the need to employ devices for setting moods, holding attention, and for the release of excess energy of young children. When a degree of excellence has been attained, listeners are comfortable, and little else is needed besides the stories. Music, a bit of poetry, or one simple song or game may be included. It is important to remember that the need for any great variance in programming is due to the holding of young children too long in a listening attitude.

Procedure: If there is no multipurpose (or meeting) room, arrange small chairs with or without low tables, or set up shop in a carpeted area, with or without pillows or sit-upons. Children seated on chairs, however, tend to have fewer mishaps and give better attention. Pillows are more popular, less expensive, more colorful--all good reasons to have them--but they maximize the possibilities for discipline problems, which should be eliminated wherever possible. A display of books may be placed near the story area, but this approach is not so necessary with the young child as it is with the older ones.

Hints: The same storyteller should meet regularly with the same group. This arrangement is important to the child because it is reassuring: there will always be at least one friend at the library. Neither time of program nor the storyteller should be changed except in a great emergency, once the best time and person have been selected.

All volunteers should be trained carefully by a professional children's librarian, preferably one who is an experienced storyteller. Volunteers could serve better, perhaps, acting as hosts, or helping individual children, or providing cookies or transportation, or by placing a fresh flower in the story area.

Showing books before--or during--story hours may be considered good teaching technique, but it does tend to create discipline problems through distraction. However, it is reported that holding a copy of the storybook gives confidence to an apprentice. If there is something that is significant enough to have to be shown, mark the place in the book with a card and share it after the story has been told. Remember only a very few children will be able to see anything that may be shown. Few storytellers need costumes, stage makeup, or elaborate sound effects.

Although a story hour is primarily a group experience in listening, the attention paid, and the assistance given to each individual child during arrival, departure, and through the choosing of books and materials to take home, will reinforce self-image, leaving a pleasant glow of acceptance and belonging.

One other important first (and too-often forgotten) is that the wise storyteller will bring other members of the staff into the planning for any programs for children. An invitation to be involved and consulted will elicit understanding and assistance that may be very much needed and appreciated.

Other Types of Programs: Most teachers and some librarians plan times for reading aloud to children, and they are most happily received by school-age groups. With young children, however, the audience should never be large. Perhaps one of the most desirable variations in the story hour is the inviting of men of different races to tell stories, or to read aloud, to boys and girls. Many youngsters do not have an opportunity in their homes to share literature with male members of their households, and this experience has a special value.

When there are guest storytellers, the regular storyteller should be present to introduce them, and to assist the audience and visitors in any way.

When storytellers who have worked almost exclusively with young children wish to expand their audience, they are inclined to add more programs of a similar nature, seldom attempting story hours for older boys and girls and adults. Apprentices, however, cannot add to their backgrounds in literature when they remain within the scope of materials most often associated with the young child, and the methods through which they are presented. The storyteller should realize that mastery of stories and adaptations of full-length books suitable for older listeners will present new experiences that will enhance one's background, develop greater self-confidence, and heighten enthusiasm. Even if one chooses, after an apprenticeship in a new area of the art, to return to the telling of stories solely to the young child, the change will prove to be gratifying and beneficial.

When in-house programs become too time-consuming and too great a strain on small library staffs, turning to a series of radio broadcasts may be a happy solution. It is a bit surprising that so few storytellers have experimented in this medium. No doubt one of the deterrents is the hesitancy to approach a program director--who might in fact be wanting just such a new program that would be presented "in the public interest. "

A study of what is scheduled on local stations at the time periods considered good choices by a storyteller is an excellent first step in putting together a story hour for radio listeners. Although a program may be planned especially for children, there will be many others who will become faithful followers. A time segment either before or after a news broadcast has been found to be most acceptable. Late afternoon or early evening spots are quite popular, and to secure one of these may take real diplomacy. The one day to be carefully avoided is Sunday. The ideal situation is a late afternoon program, before the news and sports, during the workweek.

One is dealing with approximately fifteen minutes: twelve for presentation; three for station breaks, musical signatures, acknowledgments, and announcements. A framed feature--a story within a story--is possible but not necessary. There may be some variety, but the centered-story is the important item.

After preliminary decisions have been made, material is chosen, keeping in mind the amount of time available. Sign-on, sign-off, and any incidental music that will be used in each production should be included in the tape that is to be given to the program director for consideration. A typed sheet that spells out the necessary policies--and commitments --should also be handed to the program director at the first interview. An agreement to these stipulations should be entered into by both parties. Firmness in connection with the presentation of these rules will not turn off program directors. They will be pleased that such meticulous care has gone into the planning, since this gives the station a glimpse of the expertise with which the show will be produced.

With tapes of the entire performance and a copy of the suggestions for hours for airing and other arrangements in hand, the storyteller makes, and keeps promptly, an appointment with the authorities. The storyteller should hold confidential the points on which there may be a willingness to compromise until these have to be stated. Substitutes will have already been considered and measured against possible deterrents to their use. One should keep in mind that if a particular radio station is not interested, there may be one in the next town that is.

With overall arrangements provided for, the storyteller will choose a proper introductory musical theme in keeping with the title of the show. Short selections from Debussy, Grieg, Saint-Saëns, Tchaikovsky, or MacDowell are good, but one may wish to choose some sprightly, modern theme. The

storyteller should have the entire program, including the
music, taped in advance of the date it will be aired.   The
musical theme will remain the same as long as the title of
the show is kept.

Unless the storyteller has a soundproof area in which
to work, it is better to make the tapes in the station itself
where correct facilities are available.   Several programs may
be recorded in one session.   Technicians assisting with the
taping may ask for a typed copy of the material before the
recording session.   It is the storyteller's responsibility to
comply with any request that is practicable.   Having copies
of the material--taped or typed--on file will prevent any difficulty over copyrights, and will serve as evidence if problems should arise.   Tapes of the shows should be kept by
both the sponsoring agency and the radio station.   These may
be needed to use as re-runs in case of an emergency that
would otherwise call for a cancellation.

Preparation of the story is not difficult.   Procedures
of selection--keeping the time element in mind--are the same
as for a regular story hour.   The story is generally read
into the recorder, but the reader must strive to have the
presentation as personal and as smooth as possible.   The
storyteller must visualize the listening audience; attention
should be paid to keeping the voice conversational in tone,
and as casual as when speaking to a small group.   Planned
pauses are still important, but they must be quite brief.
There should be no unplanned sounds, especially none from
the fumbling with books or the turning of the pages of a script.

Permission to use copyrighted material is sought by
the storyteller, and the correspondence for a series is fascinating.   These letters, especially, when they come from the
author, illustrator, or a member of the family, are generally
warm and friendly, quite personable.   They make good displays, and may be used in publicity for the series.   These
documents should be preserved in the files of the sponsoring
agency.

Once the program has become established, slight
changes may be made: two short stories, a bit of poetry,
an interview with a guest.   A request for letters from listeners may be made in order to learn the make-up of the
audience and the extent of the area reached.   The storyteller
may also want to involve the listeners in an art display that
bears some relevance to a particular story.

One storyteller asked for participation in a contest that offered book prizes for the best models of a proper bed for "The Princess on the Pea." It was enlightening to know how many boys and young men were interested and constructed charming beds complete with mattresses and quilts; and one contestant provided a little stool to help the princess climb into bed. In each entry, of course, there appeared the three peas of great renown. These models were displayed, stirring up much interest. Such publicity is not unpleasing to library administrators.

Contests, however, have a habit of getting out of hand, so it is important to remember that each letter should be answered; each item treated to care and safe handling. There is also the expense of mailing and prizes. Volunteers are eager to help, and when properly handled, such a contest may be a real asset.

A night program of stories prepared for adults is another way of expanding one's audience. In this type of series, selection, timing, musical preludes and any accompaniment, as well as the voice are of extreme importance. Again, letters may be sought to gauge the number of listeners and their preferences in material.

By-products of such radio programs are limitless. Librarians and laypersons alike are eager to become radio "stars." It is the professional, however, who must take the initial step. Resource people in a community can often be persuaded to tape a series of good-night tales for a small honorarium, or just for the honor. There is some fear of microphones, but the use of the tape recorder lessens the pain.

When no dates are used, and when no local announcements are included, these tapes may be provided to other agencies requesting their use. When an individual storyteller makes similar productions they may be sold after proper arrangements have been made with the holders of the copyrights.

The use of the name of the storyteller in any radio story program is, of course, left to the decision of the speaker. A bit of the magic may be lost if much attention is paid to an introduction of the performer, but some form of identification may be necessary or desirable.

If an opportunity opens for a television series, a
storyteller is most fortunate, since this is rare. To mount
a project in this medium, one must have had a variety of experiences, and possess abundant energy and imagination. Many
different skills will be needed, because an attractive script
must be created and produced. A checklist of duties, procedures, and methods to implement ideas and arrangements
should be drawn for study. The source of funds, and the
amount involved, will influence both purpose and the extent
of the presentation. It is possible, however, to stage a
creditable show with a small budget.

This is reassuring when one has an ambition to experiment with a television story hour, and there is no immediate opening. A storyteller may still plan a dynamic,
eye-catching performance, offering it to channels in the area.
Preliminary planning, in either instance, is similar.

Planning without a commitment from a channel, or
sponsor, is somewhat less exciting than when one has support,
but the experience of preparing for a future airing has value.
If the storyteller is patient, a good script will surely be given
its chance. It may be necessary, however, for the story-
teller-producer to work without remuneration until a sponsor
can be found.

Decisions concerning a total series will be made early
in the project, establishing the basic structure of the program. This will answer the questions relative to whether it
is a part of another production, or if it will be a thirty-min-
ute sustaining show originating in the local studio, as well as
to its length, additional performers, and frame.

A frame would provide continuity, and it could be
fashioned with or without a studio audience. If a studio audience of children is incorporated, one must decide on the
number to be accommodated and whether admittance will be
general or invitational. A small audience, comparable to
guest performers, is stimulating but not necessary. The
funds available will settle the question of whether or not guests
will be paid.

Such a group will need some training, and it may be
allowed to participate in planning sessions. Ideas and suggestions from a potential audience can be helpful.

The program will be sketched along the lines of a radio

production, and music, announcements, and other special
features may be added if desired. Dates, time periods, and
rehearsals will be set by the television station. Sets and
permanent visuals will also be controlled by the studio. Purpose and theme may call for a particular object such as a
chair, desk, shelves, or an "interest" area.

The storyteller will tell the stories each week, but
guests, other than members of the cast (or audience), may
be introduced, interviewed, or invited to take part in a sequence appearing in a cameo role. It should be remembered
that the production is not a talk show. While storytelling may
not be a performing art, in the strictest sense, it is a form
of communication and similar to musical and dramatic presentations.

Unless the series is being presented over a public
service network, arrangements for commercials and other
necessary breaks will have to be made. It is possible to
adapt material to these interruptions through clever transition.
When there are two or more cameras, visuals may be employed, and the picture book may come into its own. Through
the use of multiple copies of the same title, illustrations and
total format can be shown interchangeably. Too extensive a
use of visuals, however, will reduce the effectiveness of the
story. The studio staff will be glad to assist and advise in
this and other matters.

Attractive appearance and dress, of the storyteller and
other performing artists, will cut the need for costumes if
these are not required nor stipulated in the script. When a
storyteller affects a special outfit, especially if it is reminiscent of fairy godmothers or Mother Goose, the program may
be categorized, lessening its appeal to a general audience.
Material, also, should be flexible to prevent viewers from
labeling the presentation a "kiddie show." A good televised
story hour can be appealing and beneficial to a wide range
of followers.

Given that copyrighted material can be cleared, the
content of television productions is limitless. The storyteller
has access to selections in the public domain and if gifted in
writing may choose to introduce some original stories and
poems. Thirty minutes is long enough to allow for experimentation and for variety.

Television is an excellent medium for the teaching of

storytelling, also, and practitioners in the art may wish to
suggest a plan for courses to be sponsored by a college or
university.

There are many ways a storyteller may expand an audience, and one of the most exciting is to produce a film on
the subject. A bit of nudging may be necessary, but an institution or agency with state or federal funds could make a
significant contribution through supporting a project of this
type.

Other activities a storyteller may choose in the expansion of one's clientele is the designing of slide-tape shows,
recordings, lecturing and teaching. The creation of cassettes
supplementing those on the market as part of a packaged deal
for dial-a-story programs can be made at little cost.

Free-lance storytellers may also increase their visibility through belonging to organizations that can aid their
careers. A membership in the National Story League is a
good beginning. If there is no chapter in a storyteller's community, information relative to organizing one may be obtained
from the League's publication, Story Art. [1]

When storytellers are interested enough, opportunities
are innumerable; the benefits, most gratifying. Many associated professions would welcome information and demonstrations in this art whose role in teaching children to speak and
to read has never been fully understood. Ways to communicate the literary heritage to the deaf, alone, should challenge
any storyteller to continue to perfect the necessary skills and
to grow as an artist in this ancient calling. Through dedi-
cated sharing of the oral tradition with men, women, and
children, storytellers can help them to understand more fully
their differences and their likenesses, which folktales have
depicted for hundreds of generations.

NOTE

1. Story Art Magazine, 872 High Street, #5710,
Canal Fulton, Ohio, 44614.

Chapter Twelve

"... AND GLADLY TECHE...."

A knowledge of the history of storytelling and a background in folklore and short stories does not necessarily prepare one to teach this art. One must have told stories to
many groups; to have experienced various types of audiences.
There should have been confrontations with the rigors of selection and problems of maintaining discipline: these are the
trials of the apprentice. One must have experimented with
various learning methods and, even, to have met defeat, so
that when speaking to students, the instructor will understand
their fears of forgetting and their uncertainty over whether or
not they can hold a group.

The teacher must have a familiarity with the sources
of pleasing materials, and an intimate acquaintance with the
pleasures and the values of the art itself. There is a need
for qualified instructors, and one should be competent to plan,
prepare, and to conduct successful sessions for students
whether they are in formal university courses, or in workshops for volunteers.

It is regrettable that many instructors are not prac-
ticing storytellers or, if they are, that they seldom demonstrate their skills before their classes. One wonders why
this is so, since it would be more believable that instructors
might spend too much time (rather than less) in sharing tales
with those who have expressed a desire to learn this art.
Former students in formal storytelling classes complain that
instructors either do not tell enough stories or that they tell
"about" stories, never completing a single tale. It is not
true that students become discouraged and feel that they can
never tell stories so well as the teacher. A good storyteller
will be so enthusiastic that this attribute alone will stimulate
the listeners to be even better than the teacher. More important, however, is that the student is aware of the demon-
strator's pleasure; then, this experience will be sought for

oneself. Teaching through demonstration has been found to be
the best technique, the surest way, to inflame a group of apprentices. They are able to view how a professional tells
stories, to learn new materials, and to have an opportunity
to study the reactions of fellow students.

An instructor with a wide repertoire can demonstrate
special points in lecturing through the introduction of bits and
pieces of different stories and not have to pick from the air
examples of characters or situations to round out an important observation. There is nothing so stimulating to potential
storytellers as a relaxed, confident teacher who is willing to
share the total story experience.

Those planning to teach the art, however, cannot rely
on the love of literature nor an appreciation of storytelling
without having studied various methods they have seen used
in the past or have employed themselves. If these have not
appeared attractive enough, one may wish to strike out in a
new direction. Before one has gone too far along the wrong
way, some eager, bright student will be delighted to apprise
the exploring teacher of this fact.

There are certain influencing factors to be considered
and to be taken as guides in planning for classes in storytelling. These include the sponsoring agency and its purpose,
the length of the course, and the prospective participants.

The sponsoring agency may be an association, an or-
ganization offering an institute to which any member of a community may apply, or a university. Universities, colleges,
and teacher-training institutions, as well as some high schools,
have expressed a willingness to write this subject into their
curricula.

The host group will set the purpose, the eligibility of
participants, and the length of time the course will be in
progress. The storyteller-instructor will follow these regulations or decide against accepting the appointment. The
teacher should also learn whether or not a grade, based on
a written examination, is required. In storytelling, a verbal
presentation, or a research project--discussed with teacher
and class--is by far the wiser choice.

The purpose may be to train women and men to tell
stories to various community groups; to instruct recreational
assistants; or to teach skills to aides working with children

in day-care centers.   Or it may be to instruct graduate students who are preparing to be children's librarians or teachers.

The length of a course generally reflects the purpose
that is also instrumental in formulating objectives.   The
length of the course controls the scope of the material covered.   There are storytelling lectures that last an hour; there
are institutes and clinics that are scheduled for at least a
week.   Extension and regular courses in colleges and universities last from three to nine months, continuing through two
semesters.

Whatever the length, the time should be used to introduce the value of the art, and consist of information about
and demonstrations in the three main steps: selection, preparation, and presentation.   Lectures and short courses, generally, include prepared bibliographies, outlines, checklists,
and other hand-outs.   In longer, formal courses, however,
much of this material is created and compiled by the students.
When there is time, students may arrange listening and viewing sessions during which they will exhibit their skills through
filmstrips, tapes, or live presentations.

The instructor will find that the reconciling of these
factors can be accomplished best through the establishment
of objectives, the achievement of which will approximate the
goals set by the sponsoring agency.

Basic planning begins with an exploration of the availability of good materials and the equipment necessary to their
use.   These will be needed for introduction to students, in
displays, and for demonstrations.   Materials for courses not
originating in agencies that can supply them, must be borrowed
from school media centers, public libraries, or by the students who have connections with information centers whose
holdings include storytelling collections and other necessary
items.

The lecturer may also furnish books and prepared
aids.   If not, the teacher should provide several good lists
including superior reference sources, indexes, articles in
professional journals, and excerpts from some of the best
books on storytelling.

A prospectus, or outline, of the course will be of much
help, and it should carry announcements of the various re-

quirements. Explanations of written work, assigned readings, and a statement of rules and regulations will facilitate a student's understanding of what otherwise might appear nebulous.

A brief introduction to the course, and the steps in preparation of story materials, may be included. While the prospectus need not offer complete coverage of the subject, it should contain items for special study and review. This outline may also describe various methods the instructor will use: lectures, demonstrations, discussions, and practice and laboratory periods. Opportunities for work sessions with members of any team that may be working with the instructor should also appear in these pages, and the information should specify days and hours this service will be available.

The prospectus may also include certain dates when visitors will lead discussions or share stories and experiences. In short, a calendar showing all special features of the course would be a most acceptable courtesy.

So the class will not have to be disappointed, arrangements for guests and the procuring of films and other necessities should be made well in advance. Orders for any books or materials that students will be expected to purchase should be placed, in writing, with the proper stores or suppliers. Confirmation of shipment should be requested.

When facilities are accessible, the instructor should arrange for beginning students to have their first attempts videotaped. Through this means, apprentices are made aware of areas where changes and corrections are to be made. If it is impossible to have videotapes, audiotapes may be substituted. Hearing their own voices will be beneficial in pointing out the need for careful enunciation, pacing, and planned use of the pause. To elicit constructive, frank criticism, tapes may be made to allow students to hear and appraise the work of others in the class. This approach is more objective, and kinder, than asking students to be on trial in live performances before their classmates. Later, when confidence grows, the apprentice will be less shy.

When a course is of adequate length, instructors should introduce classes to the intricacies of radio and television. Visits to studios and their staffs should be scheduled and, if advisable, the experience of at least one production through each medium will be invaluable. Students in storytelling are stimulated by microphones and cameras, and they give sur-

prisingly good presentations--even during a first taping. In
no way should instructors nor technicians intimate that there
should be fear or apprehension at appearing before equipment
of any type.

If live performances are to be given before an audience
of children, publicity or invitations will need to be prepared
with the help of the sponsoring agency. The agency should
also be responsible for the safety of the children if they are
to be transported from the main facility.

Such elaborate plans as radio and television programs'
involving a live audience may not be desirable, but they should
at least be considered. The planning alone is good experience
for both apprentices and instructors. As instructors continue
to teach, they will be better able to judge the particular features that fit best into a course of study. For each new
teaching experience, the instructor will be more expert in
preparing meaningful agenda. Teachers of storytelling will
also learn the methods that work best with certain groups,
and the scope of the subject that can be included for specific
lengths of time.

Instructors in the field are asked many questions over
the years, and one question comes up more often than others:
Are there any ways to make storytelling easier? The straight
answer is another question: Easier than what? Many teachers
and librarians feel that telling stories takes too much time,
and they want to make sure they are not being denied the
knowledge of short cuts to instant success.

Professional storytellers may be aghast, but there is
one device, assuredly a dangerous gimmick, that has been
formulated and used with a degree of success. Breaking all
rules of good storytelling, the plan includes a package containing copies of several short folktales selected by the instructor. Properly duplicated, with adequate identification,
these sheets, together with a short checklist of procedures,
are handed to each participant. After introductory remarks
and an explanation, the group moves into spaces where each
may be alone and as undisturbed as possible. Thirty minutes
are allowed for this period of concentration, and it should not
be broken by coffee nor announcements. Any dissidents are
asked to leave the room at this time.

The students select one of the tales, learning it according to directions. When the time is up, the class--and the

unbelievers--reassemble, and volunteers are invited to share
their stories.   Since each member of the audience has had
the exact same instructions, selections, and length of time
for preparation, there is little sense of uneasiness.   They all
feel that they are on equal footing and after all it is just a
game!   No critique is given, but a general discussion is encouraged after the speakers have sat down.

This experiment presents a pleasant challenge that few
can resist.   The instructor, of course, has seen to it that
the speakers are protected from any built-in failures arising
from interruptions or from inadequate space.   Although this
approach is not attempted with a child-audience present, it
has been found that guests and observers are among the most
eager to participate.   Once a very attractive branch librarian,
who had come only as support for her staff, carried off top
honors.   Several years later, the instructor was told by the
administrator, and others, that the administrator had developed into a firmly addicted storyteller.

The minimum of time that should be allowed is one
hour; if there is less time available for this procedure, it
should be explained but not demonstrated with that particular
group.   During the experiment, the instructor does not leave
the area, but remains to answer individual questions, quietly.
The secret of the whole affair is to maintain a climate of
experimentation and concentration; the built-in success is the
attitude of the student.

Instructors have also seen the value, especially in
courses that must cover as much ground as possible in less
than a month, of starting students with telling stories from
the second or third day of the study.   When an instructor
waits until the lectures covering the steps of selection, telling,
and presentation have been delivered, there is little time left
for a student to practice what has been learned.

This technique is implicit in a short course in storytelling, although it may be necessary to hold conferences with
those who are unconvinced or disgruntled.   These students
should be given special attention and help.   Those who have
had some experience, also, should be offered additional aid
and extra consideration so they will not feel hindered by those
who are truly beginners.   In these instances, teachers should
take the students where they are, working even harder themselves.

Some instructors have been observed to do too much talking during class: this is still the cardinal sin of the teaching profession. It is true though that those in charge must know and practice the art and strive to stimulate others to follow their example.

Individual conferences with students will help eradicate too big a fear of audiences. Consultations over selection of material are quite important, also, since it is in this area that participants are apt to fail to excel. Any attempt to disenchant students with favorite tales, however, is to drive a wedge into their hearts.

Instructors must be diplomatic, also, in encouraging individuals to place less emphasis on certain techniques they may have developed in sharing stories with audiences. If these approaches or habits are withholding pleasure from either the teller or the listener, they ought to be modified through class discussions and demonstrations as the course progresses.

Because of the need for separate conferences and periods of private consultation, classes in storytelling should be kept small. With the exception of mini-workshops, this fact is generally accepted. With large groups it is possible to demonstrate, offer handouts of suggestions and bibliographies, and let it go at that. With enough time, one must feel one's way, allowing each student to learn at a natural pace.

When a storyteller wishes to add teaching to other expertise, there will be many opportunities to work with exciting groups. One of the most rewarding is high school juniors and seniors who are taking courses, often referred to as Homemaking, under departments of home economics. These young women--and young men have been included recently--are bright and eager to grow. They have many innovative ideas to share. They are willing to stretch and to do exceptionally good work, and they show little or no fear of children! They take instruction well, their memories are excellent, and they have great faith in the art.

When invitations to teach are slow in coming, storytellers may offer their services to agencies and institutions that may never have thought they could afford this course of study. So, get a sponsor; plan well; speed the good word.

Chapter Thirteen

"NOTHING PERSONAL, BUT NO!"

It is not enough for the storyteller to say, "Have story,
will travel." One must promote the art. Although there may
be raging battles for and against the advertising of doctors
and lawyers, there is an open, quiet field in which the professional storyteller may begin to wage a private war. Unless
there is a willingness to mount a promotional campaign for
the art in its traditional style, it may cease altogether. A
goal must be established; a blueprint drawn to guide implementation of a successful plan for attack.

The telling of stories in large public libraries in the
United States, in the early days of their histories, was, after
circulation of materials and reference services, the main effort to bring children into the fold. Children's librarians,
with encouragement from branch heads and directors of children's services (when there was one), planned a weekly story
hour. The selections were generally made during the work-
day, but the preparation was done at home on personal time.
Any small sums needed for materials or accessories to spark
the fun came from the private pocket.

This once-a-week affair lasted for about nine months
with stepped-up activity, or discontinuance, during the summer months. The programs were planned for large groups,
and were presented in an auditorium or meeting room. They
were repeated the same afternoon if not all the children could
be accommodated at a single telling. For almost two decades
this pattern held, but in the late 1930's a second kind of story
hour was introduced.

The new program was planned for preschool children,
and it was designed to share with them the exquisite, classic
picture books as well as the new ones coming available. These
groups were small, and the youngsters came together one

morning a week. With the growth of public and private kindergartens and day-care centers, the times and programs
were fashioned to meet the needs of quite young girls and
boys.

As more children were offered these regular services,
it was a strain for the existing personnel to provide meaningful experiences. Visits by children's librarians to schools in
the community were sharply curtailed. Programs for the
older boys and girls slowly dwindled, and the traditional story
hour was given less attention.

A concentration of ages, from two to five, convinced
library staffs that the week-day morning schedule called for
a change of pace from the customary folk and fairy tales.
The youngest children had not had experiences in listening,
and the older ones who had, missed the quieting influence of
their senior siblings. Too, they were fresh from infant and
Sunday schools that allowed them to sing, dance, play, and
to participate in counting games and speaking aloud. These
children were eager to move about, to help tell a story they
knew, and to share a one-to-one relationship with the children's librarian.

There were not only special activities for the children
who came in groups, but there were additional times planned
for those who did not attend any kind of preschool classes.
These sessions began to become extensions of play enjoyed
in the public and private centers, or were provided by their
families at home: songs, rhymes, games, and coloring with
crayons. The three to fives came in the mornings and, while
they were noisy in their running about, they were no longer
disruptive on busy afternoons when staffs were helping teen-
agers and adults.

Gentle pressure came from the reawakening of concepts that young children learn quickly and need contact with
music and words, and that the early establishment of habits
along these lines is partly the responsibility of professionals
in these areas. Since preparation for the many-faceted affairs took considerably more time than that spent just showing picture books, or that utilized by children's librarians who
had learned their stories at home, story programs for older
children continued to fade away.

Teaching techniques employed during World War II exhibited how the many could be taught to read quickly, and the

birth of packaged audiovisual materials soon replaced, to some
degree, even the picture book hours.   Thus, it is necessary
to rethink ways to reintroduce literature through storytelling
to all children.

The goal should be a greater visibility of the existing
programs for children six and older.   The public should be
stimulated to ask for and support the reinstatement of storytelling in cultural events in schools and libraries.   There
must be promotional efforts to renew interest in the learning
of skills in selecting materials and in listening.   Storytelling
to school-age children should not be difficult to sell to adults,
since it embodies the three thrusts being made by parents led
on by critics of public education.   It is a return to the basics,
it is innovative in that it is not now in style, and it is far
enough removed from everyday activities that the public may
believe itself to be actually inventing the whole idea.   Some
adults remember when they attended a story hour, or listened
to a media specialist, and, since it was one of the very few
extracurricular activities they were allowed to enjoy, they
remember them kindly.

With the addition of such programs, however, comes
the need for increased funding for training and presentation.
To implement a blueprint for action to acquaint various governmental agencies of this need, it will be necessary to establish exemplary programs for all age levels, to insure successful projects, and to create viable programs for study and
evaluation.

There must be personnel to write proposals that will
win approval and funds and there should be knowledgeable
storytellers to structure and set into motion superior occasions.   There should be back-up personnel.   Opportunities
for new storytellers to learn the skill should be created, and
there should be collections of books and other materials to
give substance.   Girls and boys, and adults, who become involved, will carry the word to the communities, but the public must be made aware of this return to the shoring up of
one of the three "R's."   Publicity through mass media can
easily pass the good news all along the line.

The blueprint, to aid implementation to achieve the
goals, must start with the acceptance by the administration
and the staff of the institutions and agencies that are to be
partners in the endeavor.   Chief administrators should be
presented with carefully conceived, fully-written plans so that

they may see exactly what is to be included.   The appropriate
administrator should be sought as a planning consultant as
early as practicable.

The state of the art, locally, may also be presented,
verbally and in writing, to those concerned, and should include
information anent storytelling programs in progress.   Statistical information should give scope, ages, schedules, and
numbers attending.   The strengths and weaknesses of the existing programs should be enumerated.   Trends and changes
being made in the service should reflect the greater benefits,
and they must be studied for future innovations and possible
redirection.   The position paper will also contain any new
formats in the planning stage that will upgrade present activities.   Neat figures giving suggestions for program-budgeting
and deft explanations should accompany the report.   Areas for
study, exemplary projects elsewhere, and the possibility of
extending services along cultural lines, additions to physical
facilities, and any increase in staff should be included.

Sources of funds for maintenance of the projected enlarged program should be brought to the attention of the administration.   It is well to point out that public approval of
new services to children will enhance public relations and result in goodwill for the parent agency.   For action later, but
to be noted in an early series of suggestions, there can be
proposed methods through which the public may be encouraged
to become involved as volunteers or as "friends" to serve in
consultative positions and to contribute the layperson's point
of view.

Perhaps improvements also attractive to administrators, because of their feasibility and less expensive nature,
would be the recruitment of staff who might be interested in
developing a new hobby, board members who could be persuaded to donate time, talents, and money, and a search for
an unused space that could be renovated to house an expanding program.   A request to consult with the architects and
building consultants should be made when new facilities are
being considered; especially in regard to the installation or
improvement of acoustical materials.

It should be made known that increased programs will
necessitate more thoughtful planning for space than that undertaken, or needed, to include a tiny corner (with steps) in the
already too small children's area.   These facilities should
not be located in traffic lanes that will prohibit use of any

materials and/or equipment necessary. Places for story hours should not be too close to seating or materials provided for very young children. Such will preclude any use that might be made by older boys and girls who would eventually be drawn into new programs in the oral tradition. The fear that space for children will interfere with services to adults should be laid to rest through precise planning and astute diplomacy.

Before any project is allowed to take shape, the needs and the interests of the community should be investigated, and a meeting of at least some of them should be reflected in a proposed outline of new services and activities. When a staff is knowledgeable of the community it serves, the effort involved should not be so exhaustive that all energy would go into the writing up of such a proposal. Cultural needs are not so deeply hidden that a great deal of time is needed to ascertain a firm, positive beginning.

The survey should point up what levels in respect to age must be included in the immediate plan; what new levels could be left for further identification and additional service. The study must include the various citizens not being served by any cultural units, and by all means, adults are not to be excluded: the sick, the well, the imprisoned, the old, and the poor should at least be identified for consideration. Foster homes for children; rest homes for the infirm; housing units for the elderly, and institutions serving the blind and the handicapped all are to be marked for attention.

A structured program that will promote good public relations, and will command good press, should be among the first considerations of professionals who understand the need for recreational, cultural activities that include storytelling. The administration must be convinced that any change in policy, any winning-over of the board will be feasible: that the new concepts will be acceptable if not wildly attractive.

Storytellers need the support of the administrators, they cannot go it alone. Once the authorities are acquainted with the potential of even a portion of an arrangement such as suggested, they will encourage the children's services staff to make the ideas known to other members of the library force and its associates. It is foolhardy for children's librarians to believe that they, alone, can reach this admirable and worthy goal.

Long-range plans will also include ways to encourage
more public and private colleges, teacher-training institutions,
and universities to offer training for storytellers in their curricula. Those working in many types of services for children
at both the state and national levels may be brought into the
discussions. Ultimately, a revival of storytelling cannot be
achieved without governmental support. Continuous programs
for all children will call for funds for personnel, for materials, space, and publicity.

There are at least three federal programs from which
funds are obtainable: the Elementary and Secondary Education Act, the Library Services and Construction Act, and the
National Foundation for the Arts and the Humanities. Also,
the federal government has recognized the need for an increase in cultural opportunities for the inner-city child. While
this commitment is active, the professional should grasp the
opportunity and write appealing proposals.

Private foundations could be attracted by superior
projects. Money from the private sector, already marked
for continuing education, could be tapped. Not long ago an
official for a well-known private foundation was approached
in the hopes of uncovering latent interest in the promotion of
programs in storytelling. The answer was most encouraging.
Lethargy on the part of the influential must not be taken as
a sign that enthusiasm cannot be awakened.

State consultants to public library services for children
and media specialists in departments of public instruction have
a definite role to play. They could arrange workshops in the
subject for professional librarians and teachers; schedule con-
centrica at which trustees and other guests would appear as
observers. State level personnel should also alert institutions
of higher learning concerning the need for them to offer training in the art for teachers and librarians. These consultants
can also provide incentive for the expansion of local storytelling services through regional demonstration projects and
workshops. Radio and television programs sponsored by a
state could be on loan to agencies equipped to air them.

Agencies with the proper facilities could produce films
on storytelling. "There's Something About a Story"[1] is solid
evidence of the wisdom of such a project. It has been shown
over and over with success in instructing, and involving, thousands of potential storytellers from both the professions and
the lay public.

A group of itinerant storytellers could be organized, with state leadership, which could take programs--and inspiration--into areas where there has been no activity of this nature. Several counties might be encouraged to pay the salary of a professional storyteller to serve each of them on an equal, visiting basis. This type of arrangement should not be allowed to exist for too long a time, however, since it would deter the securing of a children's librarian or the developing of local storytellers.

With the realization of ongoing, viable programs, the work of the storyteller is still not at an end. Among the most important charges of the storyteller turned promoter are encouraging the evaluation of these projects and supporting research in the field. The task of convincing governments and private foundations to allocate funds for experimentation and demonstration will go more smoothly when there are studies whose results substantiate the claims made for the need of institutional story hours.

It is not possible to write proposals containing the components of a feasible study that will be accepted for approval without the aid of experts. The gathering of facts has to be spread over many months involving visits to a number of programs and interviews with, and correspondence to, the army of workers in the services to be measured. There must be adequate money to allow the researchers to collect the data and to present an accurate appraisal of them in a solid paper.

Not for a single moment should anyone think that one person can wave a magic wand to create all these miracles. It is the responsibility of all those who have faith in the value of storytelling to recognize their personal obligation to give leadership in promotional efforts. It is not enough for a storyteller to choose, to learn, and to tell a story. One has to be aware of the functional details involved in the sharing with millions of people the lively doings of those who people the story world. All who have accepted the call to be interpreters of literature must be more than purveyors of books and materials. Storytellers should seek friends and funds for their art, but first, they have to win commitment from their own profession.

NOTE

1.   See under FILMS part of Bibliography.

Chapter Fourteen

A TELL-IN:
FESTIVAL, STORYTELLER, AND FRIEND

A popular weekly news magazine has a clever way of
introducing, through a small picture with a brief legend below, a prominent personage "and friend." It is easy to de-
cipher from the format that the editor, with tongue in cheek,
often believes the "friend" to be more intriguing than the
newsmaker. It is an apt expression to borrow because to
be a storyteller, one must have at least one friend to whom
to tell the tale. The perfect friend for this role is another
storyteller.

When the second storyteller returns the story with a
different tale, a proper tell-in results. The occasion becomes a many-sided conversation--with storytellers and wri-
ters--the storytellers taking turns as listeners. It is good
conversation, and all emerge inspired and cheered. While
one friend is necessary to round out the experience, there
is no greater pleasure than sharing stories with several storytelling friends, however strong the stress of self-conscious-
ness and the powerful motivation for speaking well before
one's peers.

Such events take several shapes. They vary in length
from a snippet of a story on a street corner to days and days
in a formal sharing. These occasions may come regularly;
they may be planned as rare, special events. Tell-ins may
be carefully structured; they may happen suddenly when two
or three come together in a single room of a hotel. Someone speaking on almost any subject may spark another storyteller. It is not difficult to understand how persons who enjoy people and literature tend to seek each other for talk, and
among storytellers this leads to tale-telling.

The sharing of stories with others caught up in the
same art may be a meticulously designed affair with commit-

tees, subcommittees, and purpose--lots of purpose. Classes
in storytelling do come to an end, and an instructor is eager
to give apprentices an opportunity to share the fun, to gather
experience in matching skills with fellow students. This exercise is somewhat similar to a graduation ceremony; it is
a prelude to the commencement of a bright new way to communicate with children and adults.

The time of day or night is set for the convenience of
both the audience and the storytellers, since they wish to invite other friends and guests. A tell-in is one of the ways a
teacher may bring to the attention of administrators and fac-
ulty the power of the art and the need to include courses in
the subject in the regular curriculum. The program may also
be set to honor a special person or event.

Storytellers sharing a tell-in are not always students.
They may be experienced artists who have come together to
refresh their spirits and to sharpen their skills, to greet old
friends, and to meet newcomers to the art. Agencies having
storytellers on their staffs often offer opportunities for such
gatherings for the purpose of in-service training. A concen-
trica--with storytellers sharing their tales with a group of
listeners--has been found to be most advantageous, since the
entertainment takes place before a second audience of observers who serve as critics and evaluators.

A combination of the best features of a tell-in was
exhibited in the honoring of several of the best loved storytellers when the American Library Association presented its
memorable program at the 1956 conference in Miami.

There are many variations; they achieve significant
objectives. One of these is to give students experience in
arranging similar events later in their own careers. These
occasions are planned to involve the entire class and the instructor, as well as any member of a team that may have
been working with the group.

Each student demonstrates how well the suggestions
and teachings of the lecturer have been received. The role
of the instructor in the planning is to encourage and to help,
but it does not include any of the actual work. The apprentices volunteer for the various tasks, and from their choices
one may learn the areas in which each is most interested.

One of the subcommittees of such an event may sur-

prise experienced storytellers: the selection committee.
When those new to the art are arranging a tell-in, it may
not be wise to ask them to present pre-selected material.
In a similar occasion for experienced storytellers, however,
it is well to have the chairperson appoint such a committee.

This group represents an audience that may have requests for specific tales. Listeners do have favorites, and
although it is monotonous to include the same story too often,
certain tales are worthy of repetition. This suggestion may
come abruptly to the person who has always been told that
selection must be left to the storyteller. This is not always
true.

A storyteller was once invited to share her storytelling
with a large audience of professional librarians. The invitation carried a request for James Thurber's Many Moons. The
tale is delightful, but an honest telling will take days of hard
work and much concentration. This selection presented a real
challenge to the storyteller, and she accepted it.

The hours of intense preparation were valuable and
bracing; the results gratifying. The listeners experienced
through the sheer force of the story itself, the amount of effort expended in its presentation. When an audience represents special interest groups, or when there are purposes in
addition to the usual one of just giving pleasure, a tell-in
should include storytellers who are willing to accept specific
requests regardless of the work involved. When the program
committee has particular selections they wish to include, the
experienced storyteller is seldom embarrassed or put to work
beyond the ordinary skills.

Hearing good storytellers share some of the stories
that may have been thought too difficult always stirs enter-
prising potential storytellers to attempt these superior tales.
Rich content for tell-ins, of course, makes them exciting,
and some well-known favorites should be included. Experienced tellers often have these in their repertoires, and they
will be glad to dust them off and share them once more.
When a request cannot be filled, the storyteller will be able
to suggest a story comparable to the rejected one.

For all the effort entailed, these special programs give
great personal satisfaction to all storytellers who thoroughly
enjoy participating in them. These occasions, clinical in nature, offer opportunities for even the best storytellers to com-

pare notes, develop new techniques, and become acquainted
with recent material.

But the most fun of all are the private, intimate presentations when children's librarians, media specialists, and
teachers--learning to tell stories--involve their roommates,
spouses, children, and neighbors.

Ruth Tooze writes of the telling of tales "near a rock
in Wales," at "crossroads in Ireland," and on "a street in
Japan."[1] There are gatherings in mountain cabins; chance
meetings with "an old music-maker of the Ute tribe in Utah"[2];
"the Basque captain," "the dirty tinker," and the chieftain of
the Onondagas of whom Sawyer wrote. [3]

Tell-ins happen all over the world, planned and spontaneous, and there are formal and regular events in Missouri,
New York, North Carolina, Oregon, and many other states.
Twosomes, also--stories shared with one very special person
--dot the history of storytelling's beginnings in this country:
Ruth and Johanna, Jane and Lily, and the child who listened
to her grandmother fashion tales of the Old South to the accompaniment of a flashing tatting shuttle, or the slip-clicking
of amber knitting needles.

Sit quietly for a moment, and conjure up the two who
sat for hours in the house in Lenox, in the Berkshires, more
than a hundred years ago. They were two authors: the younger,
a seaman in his early years, now a writer of essays, sea
tales, and adventures he had known; the older, mystic and
questioner, writing novels and books for children: The Wonder Book and Tanglewood Tales. What stories they must have
exchanged before the blazing hearth during the long winter
talks they shared. Nathaniel Hawthorne was struggling to
support his family; Herman Melville searching to find himself and to finish his Moby Dick that he would dedicate to his
friend with whom he swapped his tales.

The reader can imagine, too, a picnic and a ride on
the river, listening in as Lewis Carroll begins a story about
Alice for the delight of three little girls on July 4, 1862. The
scene shifts to a large Russian estate; another blazing hearth
against the bitter weather, and Tolstoy (busy with War and
Peace) gives a fatherly smile of approval and listens as his
friend, Ivan Turgenev, tells stories of life in Paris. [4] One
may see again, years later, thousands of miles away, the
young Stephen Crane sitting on the steps of a boarding house

and listening to the tales of soldiers, back from the war that forced brother against brother.

Following the story trail, if one is lucky, the traveler comes upon a group of storytellers listening as Hazel Richardson gives of herself and her art and shares Kipling's "The Cat That Walked by Himself." Stay for a day or a month and be with the same group as Ruth Hoey, beautiful and Irish, and "Molly Whuppie" come to live forever in the memory of those who met them on a day in spring.

Less learned, perhaps, but no less appreciative, are the knots of men around other fires as cowhands tell their tall, tall tales. And, reminiscent of those scenes, down through the years, Glen Rounds--cowhand, cook, artist and author--has sat by his fireside spinning his yarns to his friends as they listen and smell the chicken roasting in the oven near by. Not too many miles away are Manly Wade Wellman and his friends: the storytellers, the music makers, and the singers of ballads keep alive the stories of the hills and tallest peaks of Appalachia and beyond.

Great is the storyteller, greater the storytelling, but one may yearn for the best of all, a fantasy tell-in second to none. It must be fashioned for a special place. Where shall it be: in the sunken fairyland of the Butchart Gardens; on the beach at Macao; at the foot of the lions on Delos; on Poseidon's (and Byron's) hill? Any magic spot will do just as long as there's room for all--and hands reached high to be counted.

Among the storytellers of yesterday and today, at such a tell-in, one recognizes the great and the famous; the writers, collectors, and students of the art; and just storytellers and friends. One notices Chaucer and Pepys--those old, beloved gossips--and the company they keep: Joseph Jacobs, Frank Stockton, Mark Twain, and Robert Southey.

A bit of argument blurs the hearing, and there is Kipling (bless him) complaining, and wonder of wonders, of, and to: Leonardo da Vinci. Leonardo wrote "The Fox and the Magpie," and no one minded, but horrors, he also wrote "The Crocodile and the Ichneuman" and Kipling doesn't like to be reminded that Leonardo bested him, before he had ever lived or written. Kipling contends it is his mongoose that is the more famous.

Aesop smiles at them both, but he does not stay to listen. He is rounding up all the children he has taught and to whom he told his tales.   He waves to Sandburg sitting on a stone singing to his guitar.   He passes on; the storytellers are being introduced; all is quiet.

Who are they? What will they tell? Who planned this festival?   The last question could be answered in one try: Ann Caraway. [5] Here she comes now with Nicholas snug in his handbag house, and standing near are Beatrix and Peter: the four are good, good friends.   And one startling creature, gorgeous in filmy red drapery and golden turned-up shoes will tell the stories: Scheherazade, who saved her own life with her stories--she'll tell stories for many a day.

Boccaccio and Will Shakespeare will listen, as will Andersen, the pied piper of storytellers.   Socrates and his students have left the city streets to come.   Ometecutli, god of the sky and Omeciuatl, goddess of the earth (and the Aztecs) are there; Zeus and Hera--down from Olympus for the day with Homer--and, from Asgard and Gladsheim, Odin and Frigg have come to join the festival.   Truly, it is a pantheon, a company of gods.

But that blasted Kipling! The magical fellow interrupts us shouting to Homer about the poem Kipling has written, in which he has proclaimed that he, like Homer, will say and write only what pleases him.   It is a mighty gathering and the afternoon is filled with lights and shadows, enchantment, and o, so lovely mystery.

The audience of the unnamed listen and love and remember the days of sharing stories on a "Princess" of a ship making her way across to Victoria, a bicycle path on Belle Isle, a Sunday under the cypress trees in Chapultepec Park, and the night of stories with the children on the Zócalo.

For one blissful moment, like the thrum of cloth left on the loom when the tapestry is gently pulled away, there is present in one memory, the boy who hurried over at the intersection of two busy streets, to say "Tell it again."

NOTES

1. Tooze: pp. 11-13.

2. Ibid. : pp. 4-5.

3. Sawyer, The Way.... p. 44.

4. Sara Newton Carroll, The Search: A Biography of Leo Tolstoy, Harper & Row, c1973; p. 102.

5. Sayers, Anne Carroll Moore: p. 178.

BIBLIOGRAPHY
(Divided into Books, Articles, Films)

BOOKS

Aardema, Verna. Why Mosquitos Buzz in People's Ears.
Dial, 1975.

Andersen, Hans Christian. The Complete Fairy Tales and
Stories, translated from the Danish by Erik Christian
Haugaard, Foreword by Virginia Haviland. Doubleday,
c1974.

Angelo, Valenti. Nino. Viking, n. d.

Arbuthnot, May Hill. ... Anthology of Children's Literature,
rev. by Zena Sutherland. Lothrop, Lee and Shepard,
1976.

_____ Children and Books. Scott, Foresman, c1947.

_____ Time for Fairy Tales, Old and New. Scott, Foresman, 1961.

_____ Time for Old Magic. Scott, Foresman, 1970.

Association for Childhood Education International. Told Under the Magic Umbrella. Macmillan, 1939.

Bailey, Carolyn Sherwin. Stories Children Need. Milton
Bradley Co. , 1922.

Baker, Augusta, and Ellin Greene. Storytelling, Art and
Technique. Bowker, c1977.

Barringer, D. Moreau. And the Waters Prevailed. Dutton,
1956.

Bauer, Caroline Feller. Handbook for Storytellers. American Library Association, c1977.

Beecroft, John see Kipling

Benét, Stephen Vincent. Selected Works..., vol. two, Prose. Farrar, Straus & Giroux, 1942.

Bettelheim, Bruno. The Uses of Enchantment. Knopf, 1976.

Bishop, Claire Huchet. Pancakes--Paris. Viking, 1947.

_____, and Kurt Wiese. The Five Chinese Brothers. Coward, McCann and Geoghegan, 1938.

Boggs, Ralph Steele, and Mary Gould Davis. Three Golden Oranges. Longmans, Green, c1936.

Boni, Margaret Bradford. Fireside Book of Folk Songs. Simon & Schuster, 1947.

Bontemps, Arna. The Lonesome Boy. Houghton Mifflin, 1955.

Brewton, John E. Index to Children's Poetry. H. W. Wilson Co., 1942; supplements.

Brewton, Sara, and John E. Brewton. Bridled with Rainbows. Macmillan, c1949.

Briggs, Katharine. An Encyclopedia of Fairies.... Pantheon, 1977.

Brooke, L. Leslie. The Story of the Three Bears. Warne, 1934.

Bryant, Sara Cone. How to Tell Stories to Children. Houghton Mifflin, 1924; reprint, Gale, 1973.

Chase, Richard. Grandfather Tales. Houghton Mifflin, 1948.

_____ The Jack Tales. Houghton Mifflin, 1943, 1971.

Chaucer, Geoffrey. The Complete Works..., ed. by F. N. Robinson. Houghton Mifflin, c1933.

Children's Catalog, 11th ed.; 13th ed. H. W. Wilson Co., 1966; 1976.

Chrisman, Arthur Bowie. Shen of the Sea. E. P. Dutton, c1953; 1968.

Cianciolo, Patricia. Illustrations in Children's Books. William C. Brown, 1970.

Clemens, Samuel Langhorne (i. e. , Mark Twain). How to Tell a Story and Other Essays. Harper, 1897.

Coatsworth, Elizabeth. The Cat Who Went to Heaven. Macmillan, 1930.

Cole, Ann. I Saw a Purple Cow. Little, Brown, 1972.

Colwell, Eileen. A Second Storyteller's Choice. Henry Z. Walck, 1965.

_____ A Storyteller's Choice. Henry Z. Walck, 1964.

Courlander, Harold, and George Herzog. The Cow-tail Switch. Holt, Rinehart & Winston, c1947.

Davis, Mary Gould. A Baker's Dozen. Harcourt Brace, 1930.

Davison, Wilburt C. The Compleat Pediatrician. Seeman Printery, 1934.

DeJong, Meindert. Shadrach. Harper & Row, 1953.

De Maupassant, Guy. Selected Tales of.... Random House, c1950.

De Regniers, Beatrice Schenk. Little Sister and the Month Brothers. Seabury Press, 1976.

Dickinson, Asa Don, and Ada M. Skinner. The Children's Book of Christmas Stories. Doubleday, c1913.

Downs, Robert B. , ed. The Bear Went Over the Mountain. Macmillan, c1964.

Estes, Eleanor. The Hundred Dresses. Harcourt Brace Jovanovich, 1944.

Fenner, Phyllis R. Giants and Witches and a Dragon or Two. Knopf, 1943.

_____ Princesses and Peasant Boys. Knopf, 1944.

Finger, Charles J. Tales from Silver Lands. Doubleday, 1924.

Gág, Wanda. The Funny Thing. Coward, McCann and Geoghegan, 1929.

_____ Millions of Cats. Coward, McCann and Geoghegan, 1928.

Galdone, Paul. The Three Bears. Seabury Press, 1972.

Gardner, Emelyn E., and Eloise Ramsey. A Handbook of Children's Literature. Scott, Foresman, c1927.

Geisel, Theodor (Dr. Seuss). And to Think That I Saw It on Mulberry Street. Vanguard Press, 1937.

_____ The Five Hundred Hats of Bartholomew Cubbins. Vanguard Press, 1938.

Gregory, Ruth W. Anniversaries and Holidays. American Library Association, 1975. (A revision of the work by Mary Emogene Hazeltine.)

Gruenberg, Sidonie Matsner. Favorite Stories Old and New, rev. & enl. ed. Doubleday, c1955.

Hardendorft, Jeanne B. Just One More. Lippincott, 1969.

Harper, Wilhelmina. Merry Christmas to You, new rev. ed. E. P. Dutton, 1965.

Harris, Joel Chandler. Uncle Remus: His Songs and His Sayings, rev. ed. Appleton-Century-Crofts, 1921.

Haviland, Virginia. The Fairy Tale Treasury. Coward, McCann and Geoghegan, 1972.

_____ Ruth Sawyer.... Henry Z. Walck, 1965.

Hazard, Paul. Books, Children and Men. Horn Book, 1947.

Heinlein, Robert A. Citizen of the Galaxy. Scribner's, 1957.

Hogrogian, Nonny. One Fine Day. Macmillan, 1971.

Hood, Flora Mae. Something for the Medicine Man. Melmont, c1962.

Huck, Charlotte, and Doris A. Young. Children's Literature in the Elementary School. Holt, Rinehart & Winston, c1961.

Hunter, Edith Fisher. Sue Ellen. Houghton Mifflin, c1969.

Hutchinson, Veronica S. Candle-light Stories. G. P. Putnam's, 1928.

Ireland, Norma Olin. Index to Fairy Tales 1949 to 1972. F. W. Faxon, 1973.

Isherwood, Christopher, ed. Great English Short Stories, with a foreword and introduction by.... Dell, 1957.

Jacobs, Joseph. English Folk and Fairy Tales, 3d ed. rev. Putnam's, n. d.

Jagendorf, M. A. Tyll Ulenspiegel's Merry Pranks. Vanguard Press, 1938.

Jarrell, Randall. The Bat-Poet. Macmillan, 1964.

Johnson, Edna, Evelyn R. Sickels, Frances Clarke Sayers. Anthology of Children's Literature, 4th rev. ed. Houghton Mifflin, c1970.

Karl, Jean. From Childhood to Childhood. John Day, 1970.

Kipling, Rudyard. The Jungle Books, vol. 1. Doubleday, 1948.

_____ Just So Stories. Doubleday, 1932.

_____ Kipling: A Selection of His Stories and Poems, ed. by John Beecroft. Doubleday, 1956.

Korty, Carol. Plays from African Folklore. Scribner's, 1975.

Krum, Charlotte. Four Riders. Follett, 1953.

Leonardo da Vinci. Fables of..., interpreted and transcribed by Bruno Nardini. Hubbard Press, c1973.

Lionni, Leo. Inch by Inch. Ivan Obolensky (Astor-Honor), c1960.

Meigs, Cornelia, ed. , et al. A Critical History of Children's Literature, rev. ed. Macmillan, 1969.

Menotti, Gian Carlo. Amahl and the Night Visitors, adapted by Frances Frost. McGraw-Hill, 1952.

Mitchell, Lucy Sprague. Here and Now Story Book, new ed. , rev. & enl. , Dutton, c1948.

Moore, Anne Carroll. My Roads to Childhood: Views and Reviews of Children's Books. Horn Book, c1961.

Moore, Vardine. Pre-School Story Hour, 2d ed. Scarecrow Press, 1972.

Munro, H. H. see Saki

Mure, Eleanor. The Story of the Three Bears. Henry Z. Walck, 1967.

Newell, Hope. The Little Old Woman Who Used Her Head. Thomas Nelson, c1935; 1973.

Palmer, Robin. A Dictionary of Mythical Places. Henry Z. Walck, 1975.

Pellowski, Anne. The World of Children's Literature. Bowker, 1968.

_____ The World of Storytelling. Bowker, 1977.

Pyle, Howard. The Wonder Clock. Harper & Row, 1915.

Quigley, Lillian. The Blind Men and the Elephant. Scribner's, 1959.

Rawlings, Marjorie Kinnan. The Secret River. Scribner's, 1955.

Robinson, F. N. see Chaucer

Ross, Eulalie Steinmetz, ed. The Lost Half Hour.... Harcourt Brace Jovanovich, 1963.

Rufsvold, Margaret I. Guides to Educational Media. American Library Association, 1977.

Sachs, Marilyn. The Bears' House. Doubleday, 1971.

Saki (H. H. Munro). Short Stories.... Viking, 1936.

Sandburg, Carl. Rootabaga Stories. Harcourt Brace Jovanovich, 1936.

Sawyer, Ruth. The Long Christmas. Viking, 1944.

_____ My Spain: A Storyteller's Year of Collecting. Viking, 1967.

_____ This Way to Christmas. Harper & Row, c1916.

_____ The Way of the Storyteller, enl. ed. Viking, c1962 (earlier ed., 1942).

Sayers, Frances Clarke. Anne Carroll Moore. Atheneum, c1972.

_____ Summoned by Books. Viking, c1965.

Sechrist, Elizabeth Hough. It's Time for Story Hour. Macrae Smith, 1964.

Shedlock, Marie L. The Art of the Story-teller, 3d ed. rev., with a new bibliography by Eulalie Steinmetz. Dover, 1952.

Sherlock, Philip M. Anansi, the Spider Man. Crowell, 1954.

Smith, Dorothy B. Frizzell, and Eva L. Andrews, comps. Subject Index to Poetry.... American Library Association, 1977.

Steegmuller, Frances. Le Hibou et la Poussiquette. Pictures by Barbara Cooney. Little, Brown, 1959; 1961.

Steel, Flora Annie. English Fairy Tales. Macmillan, 1918, 1946, 1962.

Steele, Max. The Cat and the Coffee Drinkers. Harper & Row, 1969.

Sutherland, Zena. Children and Books, 5th ed. Scott, Foresman, 1977.

Tashjian, Virginia A. Juba This and Juba That. Little, Brown, 1969.

Thorne-Thomsen, Gudrun. Storytelling and Stories I Tell
    [a pamphlet]. Viking, 1956.

Thurber, James. Many Moons. Harcourt Brace Jovanovich,
    1943.

Tooze, Ruth. Storytelling. Prentice-Hall, c1959.

Twain, Mark see Clemens

Tyler, Anna Cogswell. Twenty-Four Unusual Stories. Har-
    court Brace Jovanovich, 1921.

Ward, Lynd. The Biggest Bear. Houghton Mifflin, c1952.

Wezel, Peter. The Good Bird. Harper & Row, 1964.

Wiggin, Kate Douglas. Tales of Laughter. McClure, Phil-
    lips, 1908.

Wilde, Oscar. The Happy Prince. Dutton, 1968.

Zemach, Harve. Duffy and the Devil. Farrar, Straus &
    Giroux, 1975.

Ziegler, Elsie. Folklore.... F. W. Faxon, 1973.

Ziskind, Sylvia. Telling Stories to Children. H. W. Wilson
    Co., 1976.

ARTICLES

Britton, Jasmine. "Gudrun Thorne-Thomsen: Storyteller
    from Norway." Horn Book Magazine, February, 1958.

Filstrup, Jane Merrill. "The Enchanted Cradle: Early Story-
    telling in Boston." Horn Book Magazine, December, 1976.

Laughton, Charles. "Storytelling." Atlantic Monthly, June,
    1950, pp. 71-73.

Sayers, Frances Clarke. "Review of The Flowering Dusk."
    Horn Book Magazine, May, 1945.

Schwartz, Albert V. "The Five Chinese Brothers: Time to
    Retire." Interracial Books for Children Bulletin, no.
    3, issue of vol. 8, 1977.

Shaw, Spencer. "Recorded Magic for Story Hours." <u>Top of</u>
     <u>the News</u>, October, 1958, pp. 43-47.

FILMS

"Art of Telling Stories to Children." University of Michigan,
     Ann Arbor; n.d. , 27 min. , color.

"Hello, Up There." Learning Corporation of America, 1350
     Avenue of the Americas, New York, N.Y.   10019;
     1970, 8 min. , color.

"Hopscotch." Churchill Films, 662 N. Robertson Blvd. , Los
     Angeles, Ca.   90069; 1973, 12 min. , color.

"The Pleasure Is Mutual." CBC, 1966.   Children's Book
     Council, 175 Fifth Avenue, New York, N.Y. ,   10010;
     24 min. , color.

"Reach Out." Filmfair Communications, 10900 Ventura Blvd. ,
     Studio City, Ca.   91604; 1971, 5 min. , color.

"There's Something About a Story." Connecticut Films, Inc. ,
     6 Cobble Hill Road, Westport, Ct. , 06880; 1969, 27
     min. , color.

INDEX

149

Ethnic groups in America viii
Everyman vii
Experimentation in use of the
taperecorder 38
Eye contact see Telling a
story, eye contact in

Fables 82; versions of viii
The Fairy Tale Treasury
(Haviland) 96
Far West, Storytelling in 72
Favorite Stories Old and New
(Gruenberg) 28
Federal funding and informa-
tion centers 29
Fenner, Phyllis R. 28
Festival, The Storytelling,
American Library Associa-
tion, Conference, June 1956,
Miami Beach, Florida 74-
75,132
Festivals, storytelling, and
tell-ins see Tell-ins
Field, Rachel 101
Film showings 91
Fink, Mike see Mike Fink
Fireside Book of Folk Songs
(Boni) 96
The Five Chinese Brothers
(Bishop and Wiese) 5,30;
target of prejudice 32
"The Five Chinese Brothers:
Time to Retire" (Schwartz)
32
The Five Hundred Hats of Bar-
tholomew Cubbins (Geisel)
27
Flannel board presentations
90
The Flowering Dusk (Young)
73
Folk humor, American, oral
xii
"Folklore" (Carmer) xii
Folklore... (Ziegler) 96
Folklore, American viii;

biological phenomena ix
Folklore, Ancient and med-
ieval, mythological crea-
tures ix
Folklore, Study of 97
Folklore and recurring pat-
terns of behavior 4
Folklore and storytelling
see Oral tradition
Folktales and ballads, geo-
graphical distribution of
vii
Forsyth County Public Li-
brary (Winston-Salem,
North Carolina) 24
Four Riders (Krum) 11
"The Fox and the Magpie"
(Leonardo da Vinci) 135
Francis Parkman Regional
Library (Detroit Public
Library, Detroit, Michi-
gan) 72
Franklin, Benjamin xii,17
Free-lance storytellers 85,
116
Frigg 136
"The Frog Prince" 4
From Childhood to Childhood
(Karl) 96
Frost, Frances 103
The Funny Thing (Gág), a
synopsis 42-43; used in
learning stories 41-44

"G. N. " 82
Galdone, Paul 44,83
"Galoshes" (Bacmeister) 101
Gardner, Emelyn E. 70
Geisel, Theodor (Dr. Seuss)
101
Gesta Romanorum vii
Gestures 43-44,47-48,52-
53,54; importance of
hands 52-53; See also
Mimicry; Pantomime
Giants and Witches and a